CIPS STUDY MATTERS

CW01669145

CERTIFICATE
PROCUREMENT AND SUPPLY OPERATIONS

COURSE BOOK

Procurement and supply functions

Printed and distributed by:

The Chartered Institute of Purchasing & Supply, Easton House, Easton on the Hill, Stamford, Lincolnshire
PE9 3NZ
Tel: +44 (0) 1780 756 777
Fax: +44 (0) 1780 751 610
Email: info@cips.org
Website: www.cips.org

First edition September 2012

Contents

Preface

Welcome to your new Course Book.

Your Course Book provides detailed coverage of all topics specified in the unit content.

For a full explanation of how to use your new Course Book, turn now to page ix. And good luck in your studies!

A note on style

Throughout your Course Book you will find that we use the masculine form of personal pronouns. This convention is adopted purely for the sake of stylistic convenience – we just don't like saying 'he/she' all the time. Please don't think this reflects any kind of bias or prejudice.

September 2012

The Unit Content

The unit content is reproduced below, together with reference to the chapter in this Course Book where each topic is covered.

Unit purpose and aim(s)

On completion of this unit, candidates will be able to identify:

(a) The main types of organisations
(b) The main elements of a procurement and supply function
(c) The main market factors and their impact on the procurement and supply function

Learning outcomes, assessment criteria and indicative content

		Chapter
1.0	**Know the main types of organisations and how they operate**	
1.1	Identify the main types of organisations	
	• Private, public and third sector organisations	**1**
	• Production and service organisations	**1**
1.2	Describe how organisations operate	
	• People, objectives and structure in organisations	**2**
	• The formal and informal organisation	**2,3**
1.3	Identify the main operating functions within organisations	
	• Differentiation and integration in organisations	**3**
	• Typical functions in organisations such as production, operations, marketing and sales, customer support, human resources, personnel, finance, IT, and technical functions	**3**
	• Differentiating procurement and supply	**3**
2.0	**Know the main elements of a procurement and supply function**	
2.1	Describe the use of mission and vision statements and objectives by a procurement and supply function	
	• Objectives of procurement and supply functions	**4**
	• Targets for procurement and supply functions	**4**
	• Use of mission and vision statements for procurement and supply functions	**4**
2.2	Describe the main roles and structures of a procurement and supply function within an organisation	
	• Links to organisational goals	**5**
	• Competition and regulatory roles	**5,6**
	• Advice and guidance that a procurement and supply function can provide to other functions	**5**
	• Procurement and supply as a service function	**5**
	• Centralised, devolved and lead buying structures of procurement and supply functions	**5**

How to Use Your Course Book

Organising your study

'Organising' is the key word: unless you are a very exceptional student, you will find a haphazard approach is insufficient, particularly if you are having to combine study with the demands of a full-time job.

A good starting point is to timetable your studies, in broad terms, between now and the date of your assessment. How many subjects are you attempting? How many chapters are there in the Course Book for each subject? Now do the sums: how many days/weeks do you have for each chapter to be studied?

Remember:

- Not every week can be regarded as a study week – you may be going on holiday, for example, or there may be weeks when the demands of your job are particularly heavy. If these can be foreseen, you should allow for them in your timetabling.
- You also need a period leading up to the assessment in which you will revise and practise what you have learned.

Once you have done the calculations, make a week-by-week timetable for yourself for each paper, allowing for study and revision of the entire unit content between now and the date of your assessment.

Getting started

Aim to find a quiet and undisturbed location for your study, and plan as far as possible to use the same period each day. Getting into a routine helps avoid wasting time. Make sure you have all the materials you need before you begin – keep interruptions to a minimum.

Using the Course Book

You should refer to the Course Book to the extent that you need it.

- If you are a newcomer to the subject, you will probably need to read through the Course Book quite thoroughly. This will be the case for most students.
- If some areas are already familiar to you – either through earlier studies or through your practical work experience – you may choose to skip sections of the Course Book.

The content of the Course Book

This Course Book has been designed to give detailed coverage of every topic in the unit content. As you will see from pages vii–viii, each topic mentioned in the unit content is dealt with in a chapter of the Course Book. For the most part the order of the Course Book follows the order of the unit content closely, though departures from this principle have occasionally been made in the interest of a logical learning order.

Each chapter begins with a reference to the assessment criteria and indicative content to be covered in the chapter. Each chapter is divided into sections, listed in the introduction to the chapter, and for the most part being actual captions from the unit content.

All of this enables you to monitor your progress through the unit content very easily and provides reassurance that you are tackling every subject that is assessable.

Each chapter contains the following features.

- Clear coverage of each topic in a concise and approachable format
- A chapter summary
- Self-test questions

The study phase

For each chapter you should begin by glancing at the main headings (listed at the start of the chapter). Then read fairly rapidly through the body of the text to absorb the main points. If it's there in the text, you can be sure it's there for a reason, so try not to skip unless the topic is one you are familiar with already.

Then return to the beginning of the chapter to start a more careful reading. You may want to take brief notes as you go along.

Test your recall and understanding of the material by attempting the self-test questions. These are accompanied by cross-references to paragraphs where you can check your answers and refresh your memory.

The revision phase

Your approach to revision should be methodical and you should aim to tackle each main area of the unit content in turn. Re-read your notes. Then do some question practice. The CIPS website contains many past exam questions and you should aim to identify those that are suitable for the unit you are studying.

Additional reading

Your Course Book provides you with the key information needed for each module but CIPS strongly advocates reading as widely as possible to augment and reinforce your understanding. CIPS produces an official reading list of books, which can be downloaded from the bookshop area of the CIPS website.

To help you, we have identified one essential textbook for each subject. We recommend that you read this for additional information.

The essential textbook for this unit is *Purchasing and Supply Chain Management* by Kenneth Lysons and Brian Farrington.

CHAPTER 1

The Main Types of Organisations

Assessment criteria and indicative content

1.1 Identify the main types of organisations

- Private, public and third sector organisations
- Production and service organisations

3.1 Identify the key economic sectors that impact on a procurement and supply function

- Public, private and not for profit or third sector

Section headings

1 Defining and classifying organisations
2 Defining the public sector
3 Private and public sectors compared
4 Third sector organisations
5 Key features of third sector procurement
6 Production and service organisations

1 Defining and classifying organisations

Defining organisations

1.1 We come across 'organisations' many times every day, and the word is very commonly used in conversation and in printed text. But what exactly do we mean by 'organisation'? How can the term be defined? What features must be present before we can say 'yes – that is an organisation'?

1.2 In some cases the absence of a clear definition might pose no problem. For example, few people would disagree with the following examples of organisations.

- A multinational company such as General Motors
- A government department such as the Department for Work and Pensions in Britain
- A charity such as Oxfam
- A university
- A professional body such as the Chartered Institute of Purchasing and Supply.

1.3 However, the need for a definition, or for a defining list of characteristics, becomes apparent in less clear-cut cases. Consider the following examples.

- A village cricket team
- A professional football club
- A school chess club
- A self-employed plumber selling his services as a 'one-man band'

- A family unit – say, a mother and father plus two young children
- A market stall run by a family – say, a mother and father plus their two teenage children

1.4 One standard text – *Organisational Behaviour* by Andrzej Huczynski and David Buchanan – offers a broad definition of organisations: '... social arrangements for the controlled performance of collective goals'.

1.5 Huczynski and Buchanan's definition suggests that the difference between organisations and other social groupings with collective goals (the family, for example) is:

- the pre-occupation with performance
- the need for controls to ensure that performance goals are being met.

1.6 The collective goals of a business organisation might include a wide range of objectives such as: profitability, market standing or market share, productivity (efficient use of resources), innovation or social responsibility (compliance with law, ethical values and/or community expectations). Typically, senior managers will lay down strategic objectives to provide overall purpose and direction for the long term. These must then be translated into more detailed operational objectives, providing a framework within which teams and individuals can make their short-term decisions day to day.

Different ways of classifying organisations

1.7 There are various ways of classifying organisations involved in procuring goods and services.

- By *structure and ownership,* including issues of incorporation (the legal structure of the organisation), ownership, control and funding. On this basis, the economy is often divided into the private sector (eg business companies), the public sector (eg government, health authorities, police and defence forces), and the third sector: sometimes subdivided into the voluntary sector (eg churches and charities) and subscription-paid sector (eg clubs, societies and associations).
- By *primary objective.* Profit-oriented organisations (common in the private sector) aim to generate profits for their owners, or return on investment. Not-for-profit organisations (common in the public and third sectors) aim to provide public, social or charitable services, protect stakeholder interests or fulfil the purposes of their members – without aiming to make a profit from doing so. Any 'surplus' of funds is reinvested in the organisation's activity.
- By *activity:* extraction of raw materials, generation of energy, manufacturing, retail, health care, information technology, media and so on. Organisations performing different activities are likely to have different objectives, technologies and practices, in order to meet the particular challenges of their task and environment.
- By *size:* special categories are often given, for example, to small and medium enterprises (SMEs) at one end of the scale and multinational corporations (MNCs) at the other.

1.8 We will look briefly at some of these distinctions and their impact on procurement and supply chain operations in this chapter.

The private and public sectors

1.9 As most readers will be aware, a private sector organisation is one that is owned by private individuals, either few in number (such as a small family business) or very numerous (as with a large company owned by millions of private shareholders). Public sector organisations on the other hand are 'owned' by the public in general.

1.10 We will look at both sectors in detail in this chapter, but some key differences between them can be summarised as follows.

1.11 In the *private sector*:

- Organisations are owned by their investors (owner/proprietors or shareholders), and controlled by directors or managers on their behalf
- Activity is funded by a combination of investment, revenue (from the sale of goods or services) and debt (eg borrowing from banks)
- The primary purpose is the achievement of commercial objectives: generally, maximising profits for their owners, or for reinvestment in the business. Managerial decisions are assessed on the extent to which they contribute to organisational profit or shareholder wealth.
- Competition is a key factor. Several, or many, firms may offer goods or services of a particular type, with consumers free to choose between their offerings. Consumer choice ensures that quality and efficiency are maintained at an acceptable level.
- The core 'constituency' served by firms is shareholders, customers and employees, all of whom are involved with the firm by choice. Firms can and must, therefore, focus their activity on meeting the needs of these few key stakeholders.

1.12 In the *public sector:*

- Organisations are owned by the government on behalf of the State, which represents the public.
- Activity is financed by the state, mainly by means of taxation – as well as any revenue the organisation's activities may generate.
- The primary purpose is achieving defined service levels: providing efficient and effective services to the public, often within defined budgetary constraints and sustainability strategies.
- There has traditionally been little or no competition, although many governments have sought to introduce some market disciplines (eg competitive tendering). In the absence of consumer choice, quality and efficiency are imposed by mechanisms such as regulation, customer charters, performance targets and competition for funding allocations.
- The 'constituency' of concerned stakeholders is wider and more diverse, including government, taxpayers, funding bodies, those who consume services – and society as a whole. There is a far greater need for accountability and stakeholder consultation in managing the organisation.

The size and scope of the different sectors

1.13 Looking at the big picture, economic activity can't produce *everything* that might conceivably be wanted or needed by consumers, because the resources to do so (the 'factors of production': land, natural resources, labour, capital and knowledge) are limited. Some mechanism is required to decide how these resources should be used, and what goods and services should be produced.

1.14 A **market economy** operates on the basis of supply and demand: people will purchase goods and services to satisfy their wants and needs, at a price they are able and willing to pay. Commercial organisations have to offer goods and services which are in demand, at prices which maintain that demand, in order to compete with others in the market. In other words, consumer choice decides which goods and services are produced, and at what price they can be sold. This has been the basis of the private sector, ever since commerce began with barter and trade in ancient rural economies.

1.15 However, some goods and services are perceived as essential for the wellbeing of individuals and society – such as health, education, utilities and security services – even if commercial organisations don't want to produce them, because consumers are unwilling or unable to pay the market price. In such circumstances (ie when the market mechanism of supply and demand 'fails') government must step in to control production, funded by taxation and public borrowing, so that basic goods and services are available to everyone on a free or subsidised basis. This is the basis of the public sector. In its extreme form (a *centrally planned economy),* the government would control all factors of production: all business would be publically owned or 'nationalised'.

1.16 A **mixed economy** is one in which there is neither complete capitalist control nor complete government control of resources. Instead, the state controls essential public services and basic industries which cannot raise adequate capital investment from private sources, while at the same time supporting private enterprise and the open market in other fields.

1.17 The functions of the public sector in a mixed economy are therefore as follows.

- To provide essential goods and services which might not be provided by the private sector, owing to 'market failure'
- To redistribute wealth, via taxation, in order to provide financial support for non-wage earners such as the sick, pensioners and the unemployed
- To regulate private sector activity in the public interest
- To 'bail out' private enterprises, where necessary in the public interest.

1.18 The balance of a mixed economy – and therefore the relative size and scope of the public or private sector – will depend partly on political factors. Communist or socialist governments (as in Cuba, China, Sweden or Norway) are more likely to support a large public sector, with government expenditure representing a higher proportion of the GDP. Capitalist societies with conservative governments are more likely to reduce the public sector (eg by privatisation of public services and industries). In highly committed 'free enterprise' economies, such as Japan and the USA, few services are provided by the state.

The third sector

1.19 As we noted earlier, the primary objective of most public sector organisations is the delivery of services, rather than the generation of profits. A number of organisations in the private sector are also operated on a not-for-profit (NFP) basis, including: charities, churches, private schools and hospitals, political parties, museums, clubs and associations, interest groups and pressure groups, trade unions and professional bodies such as CIPS. These are often identified separately as the 'third' sector of the economy (the first two being the private and public sectors).

1.20 Organisations in this sector have typically been set up to achieve a defined objective (eg for a charitable purpose or to represent the interests of a group of people) rather than to maximise profit. They usually derive their income from donations, legacies (money left to the organisation in someone's will), sponsorships and government grants and subsidies, although they may also have a trading arm to generate revenue (as in the case of 'charity shops', say). They may be owned by their members (as in a club or association) or by a trust (as in a charity), and managed by a board of trustees or directors.

1.21 We will look at the third sector separately later in this chapter.

2 Defining the public sector

Types of organisations in the public sector

2.1 There are several different types of public sector organisation.

- **Government departments** carry out the work of central government. They are financed mostly by taxation revenue.
- **Local government authorities** carry out the work of local service administration, financed by revenue raised predominantly from local sources.
- **Quasi-Autonomous National Government Organisations** (QUANGOs) are set up by the government as independent (non-departmental) bodies, which are nevertheless dependent on the government for their existence. UK examples include the Environment Agency, the Competition Commission and the Equality and Human Rights Commission. (In the US, QUANGO stands for Quasi-Autonomous *Non* Governmental Organisation, and you may see this version used in some text books.)
- **Public corporations** are state-owned industrial and commercial undertakings. They are run by a board accountable to the Secretary of State of a sponsoring government department, with which they agree their strategic objectives, performance targets and funding.
- **Municipal enterprises** are providers of goods and services (eg leisure services, museums, parks), run by local government authorities – often in competition with the private sector. Increasingly, local councils are creating separate companies or trusts to deliver such services, allowing partnership with private investors and providers.

Financing the public sector

2.2 All sources of public sector funding derive ultimately from the taxpayer. Funds are collected in various different forms: direct taxes (taxes on income, such as the corporation tax paid by companies and the income tax paid by individuals); indirect taxes (ie taxes on expenditure, such as sales tax and excise duties); and local taxes (such as council tax and business rates).

2.3 In the UK, most of this income is collected by central government (although some of it, such as council tax, is collected by local authorities). It is the task of government, and specifically the Treasury department, to distribute the income for use in the areas prioritised by government policy. If you are not based in the UK, you should investigate which authorities in your country are responsible for collecting tax.

2.4 Government agencies are provided with funds by central government for spending on their allotted responsibilities. In some cases, such agencies act as industry regulators, and when this happens, another source of their income comes from levies on the companies operating in that sector.

2.5 Where funds are collected locally, they are also spent locally, on services such as policing, rubbish collection, road maintenance and so on.

The functions of public sector organisations

2.6 The primary objectives of the public sector are *not* to make economic surplus or profits, but instead:

- To deliver essential public **services** (such as housing, healthcare, sanitation, transport, education, policing and defence) which the market might not otherwise provide equitably or fairly – to an acceptable level or quality (as expressed in government policies and customer charters)

- To encourage **national and community development**: developing education and skilling; stimulating economic activity and employment; developing technology and infrastructure (roads, communications, public spaces and so on); maintaining national security; preserving national and community heritage (both natural and human-made); supporting diversity and social inclusion (access to the benefits and opportunities offered by society); and so on
- To pursue **socio-economic goals** such as support for small and minority-owned businesses; the legislation of minimum standards for human, civil and labour rights; the promotion of work-life balance and public health; the pursuit of sustainable development, production and consumption (including sustainable procurement); environmental protection; and so on. This is often called 'corporate social responsibility' in the private sector.

2.7 A procurement vision for local councils might include six key principles, reflecting these key objectives.

- Better quality services through sustainable partnerships (ie service commissioning)
- A mixed economy of service provision (ie partnering with the private and third sectors to deliver services), with ready access to a diverse and competitive range of suppliers
- Achieving continuous improvement by collaborating with partners
- Greater value from a corporate procurement strategy
- Realising community benefits
- Stimulating markets and driving innovation in the design, construction and delivery of services

3 Private and public sectors compared

3.1 Although the private sector is the focus of most procurement and supply chain literature – and arguably represents best practice in some areas of procurement and supply – the public sector is an important context for procurement operations. The spending power of public sector enterprises is enormous, and despite widespread programmes of privatisation in most developed economies, the sheer range of public sector service provision is vast: including roads, law and order, education, health and leisure services, emergency services, defence and much more.

3.2 Public and private sector organisations and environments are different in some key respects, as we noted above. The key implications for procurement have been summarised by Gary J Zenz (*Purchasing and the Management of Materials),* whose analysis forms the basis of Table 1.1, with our own points added.

1

Table 1.1 *Differences between public and private sector purchasing*

AREA OF DIFFERENCE	PRIVATE SECTOR	PUBLIC SECTOR
Objectives	Usually, to increase profit	Usually, to achieve defined service levels
Responsibility	Buyers are responsible to directors, who in turn are responsible to shareholders	Buyers are responsible ultimately to the general public
Stakeholders	Purchasing has a defined group of stakeholders to take into account.	Purchasing has to provide value to a wider range of primary and secondary stakeholders.
Activity or process	Organisational capabilities and resources used to produce goods and services	Add value through supply of outsourced or purchased products and services. (Tend not to purchase for manufacture.)
Legal restrictions	Activities are regulated by company law, employment law, product liability law etc	Most of this applies equally to public sector, but additional regulations are present too
Competition	There is usually strong competition between many different firms	There is usually no competition
Value for money	Maintain lowest cost for competitive strategy, customer value and profit maximisation	Maintain or improve service levels within value and cost parameters.
Diversity of items	Specialised stock list for defined product and service portfolio.	Wide diversity of items and resources required to provide diverse services (eg local government authority).
Publicity	Confidentiality applies in dealings between suppliers and buyers	Confidentiality is limited because of public interest in disclosure
Budgetary limits	Investment is constrained only by availability of attractive opportunities; funding can be found if prospects are good	Investment is constrained by externally imposed spending limits
Information exchange	Private sector buyers do not exchange information with other firms, because of confidentiality and competition	Public sector buyers are willing to exchange notes and use shared e-purchasing platforms, consolidate purchases etc.
Procurement policies and procedures	Tend to be organisation-specific. Private sector buyers can cut red tape when speed of action is necessary	Tend to follow legislative directives. Public sector buyers are often obliged to follow established procedures
Supplier relationships	Emphasis on long-term partnership development where possible, to support value chain	Compulsory competitive tendering: priority to cost minimisation and efficiency, at the expense of partnership development

3.3 The differences between public and private sector purchasing should not be overemphasised, however. Differences in objectives, organisational constraints and so on may not necessarily lead to differences in operational *procedure*.

- Public sector buyers may not be seeking to maximise profit, for example, but they will still be concerned to achieve value for money.
- Public sector buyers may not seek competitive advantage, but they will still aim to ensure the quality of inputs in order to support the quality of outputs (to fulfil the terms of a customer charter, say).
- Meanwhile, private sector buyers may not have non-economic goals as their primary

objective, but they are increasingly being challenged to consider the interests of wider stakeholders in society (through pressure for corporate social responsibility).

3.4 An article in *Procurement Professional* journal (CIPS Australia) once noted that: 'Key issues for the procurement profession... are as relevant for the public sector as they are for the private sector... Work is currently underway in public sectors around the world to address these issues, centred on:

- Developing standards for the assessment and ongoing development of public procurement professionals
- The greater application of strategic sourcing principles to public procurement
- The introduction of e-procurement systems.'

3.5 There is increasing best practice sharing between sectors, with best practice models and recommendations published by public sector bodies and with commitment from the public sector to learn from private sector best practice (in areas such as closer supplier relationships, supply chain innovation and procurement professionalism).

3.6 Key priorities, such as corporate social responsibility, sustainability, customer service improvement and the reduction of cost inefficiencies, operate across sectoral boundaries.

4 Third sector organisations

The not for profit (NFP) sector

4.1 The 'third sector' of an economy comprises non-governmental organisations (NGOs) which are operated on a not-for-profit (NFP) basis, generally reinvesting any 'surplus' from their activities to further social, environmental, cultural or other value-driven objectives. Such organisations include: charities, churches, political parties, museums, clubs and associations, co-operatives, interest, pressure and advocacy groups, trade unions and professional bodies such as CIPS.

The voluntary and subscription sectors

4.2 NFP organisations are sometimes subdivided into further sectors, according to their membership and funding.

- In the **voluntary sector** (eg churches, charities and interest groups), the organisations are generally controlled by a few individuals (eg trustees), but operate by voluntary contributions of funding (eg donations and grants, plus sales of product where relevant) and participation (volunteer labour). The funds are used to maintain the work.
- In the **subscription paid sector** (eg clubs, trade unions and professional bodies), the organisations are owned by the people who pay subscriptions to be members.

Objectives of third sector organisations

4.3 Obviously, the range of third sector organisations is very wide, and they may have a range of different specific purposes.

- Raising public awareness of a cause or issue (eg environmental or social pressure and interest groups)
- Political lobbying and advocacy on behalf of a cause, issue or group
- Raising funds to carry out activities (perhaps using commercial operations to generate profits, in addition to requesting grants, donations or subscriptions)

- Providing material aid and services to the public or specific beneficiaries (eg homeless or aged care charities, wildlife protection and conservation groups)
- Providing services to members (eg trade unions advocating employment rights, and professional bodies securing ethical and technical standards)
- Mobilising and involving members of the public in community projects, for mutual benefit (eg Volunteer Service Overseas).

4.4 As with public sector organisations, the range of an NFP organisation's stakeholders can therefore be wide, including: contributors (staff, volunteers, members, donors); funding bodies (sponsors, funding authorities); beneficiaries of the services or activities; the media (since activities are often 'in the public interest'); and regulatory bodies (such as the Charities Commission in the UK). This means that there will be multiple influences on organisational policy and decision-making.

4.5 In order to avoid loss of direction, or pressure to change direction from influential stakeholders (especially sponsors and donors), third sector organisations generally set out their objectives, policies, rules and regulations in some form of governing documents – similar to the Articles of Association of a corporation. These may take the form of a written constitution, charter, trust deed or memorandum and articles of association, setting out:

- The purpose and objectives of the organisation
- Governing principles, policies, rules and regulations for operation
- Responsibilities for management of the organisation (eg the board of trustees)
- Protocols for changing administrative provisions or ceasing operations.

4.6 Johnson, Scholes & Whittington (*Exploring Corporate Strategy)* summarise some of the key characteristics of the third sector as follows: Table 1.2.

Table 1.2 *Key characteristics of the third sector*

Objectives and expectations	• May be multiple service objectives and expectations • Expectations of funding bodies are usually very influential • May be subject to political lobbying • Multiple influences on policy: complicates strategic planning • Consultation and consensus-seeking becomes a major activity • Decision-making can be slow
Market and users	• Beneficiaries of services are not necessarily contributors of revenue or resources • Multiple stakeholders and customers • Service satisfaction is not measured readily in financial terms
Resources	• Multiple sources of funding • High proportion from sponsors and donors • Resources received in advance of service delivery, often with attached expectations • Tends towards strategic emphasis on financial or resources efficiency rather than service effectiveness • Strategies and communications may be addressed as much towards sponsors and donors as clients

4.7 You may like to browse the websites of some NGOs in areas that interest you, and see how clearly articulated their values and objectives are, and how these flow down to procurement, sourcing and corporate social responsibility policies.

5 Key features of third sector procurement

Public accountability

5.1 A significant factor affecting procurement in NFP organisations is that they are seen as performing a 'stewardship' function. That is, they are spending money that has been derived not from the organisation's own trading efforts, but from someone else's donations or taxes. In fact, funding will often come from persons or organisations not themselves benefiting from the services provided.

5.2 Procurement functions are therefore more closely scrutinised and regulated than in the private commercial sector, with a strong emphasis on accountability and stewardship.

5.3 Johnson, Scholes & Whittington *(Exploring Corporate Strategy)* argue that this may cause a focus on resource efficiency at the expense of service effectiveness. In other words, there is a danger that such organisations will be less concerned to identify and satisfy the needs of their 'customers' – and more concerned with demonstrating absence of waste in their use of sponsors' funds.

5.4 Third sector organisations generally establish clear governance structures for their management – and procurement – in order to provide clarity, accountability, checks and controls on the use of funds.

Regulations impacting on charities

5.5 Third sector organisations are subject to the same general laws and regulations as other private enterprises, as discussed earlier. But they may also be subject to additional regulation, as we will illustrate in the case of charities in England and Wales. (If you are not based in England or Wales you should investigate which body regulates charities in your own country.)

5.6 The Charities Commission is the statutory regulatory body for charities in England and Wales. Its objectives (as stated on its website: www.charity-commission.gov.uk) are as follows.

- To register charities (in a similar way to the registration of companies)
- To ensure that charities meet the legal requirements for being a charity (in order to register with the Commission), and are equipped to operate properly and within the law
- To check that charities are run for public benefit, and not for private advantage
- To ensure that charities are independent and that their trustees take their decisions free of control or undue influence from outside agencies
- To detect and remedy serious mismanagement or deliberate abuse by or within charities
- To work with charities and other regulators, to enhance public confidence in charities and the work they do (in order to ensure continuing volunteer labour and funding).

5.7 The Commission has a range of responsibilities, including:

- Gathering and maintaining information about charities on the charities register, and making information available to the general public on request
- Offering advice and guidance to charities (via a help line and site visits) on governance and compliance
- Auditing charity activities to check governance and compliance arrangements
- Investigating complaints about charities, and – in the case of mismanagement or abuse – intervening to protect the charity's assets.

What do third sector organisations buy?

5.8 With such a wide range of activities carried out by third sector organisations, the range of items procured may be correspondingly wide.

- An NFP organisation may provide services – in which case, its requirements will be the same as those for other service organisations.
- An NFP organisation may have a retail arm, in order to help it raise funds – in which case, its requirements will be the same as those for other retail organisations.
- More generally, NFP organisations will have general operating requirements: office supplies and equipment, IT support, premises management services and so on.
- More specifically, NFP organisations may have requirements for specialist supplies related to their activities. A church will need premises, furniture and supplies for its religious services, say. A charity may need collecting tins, volunteer badges, merchandise for sale and so on.

Key drivers for third sector procurement policy

5.9 Key drivers for procurement policy in third sector organisations therefore include the following.

- The values of internal and external stakeholders (including founders, staff, voluntary workers, donors and supporters), which are often directly related to the mission and purpose of the organisation. This means that there will be multiple influences on procurement policy and objectives.
- The need to align procurement policies and procedures with the core values, cause, issue or theme promoted by the organisation (eg to support 'green' procurement, if the organisation is an environmental charity or lobbying group).
- The management of reputation and reputational risk. Public relations crisis, caused by some internal failure of policy or implementation, is both more likely for third sector organisations (because of the extent of scrutiny and high standards) and more significant in its impact (because of the dependence on volunteer labour, political support and discretionary funding – most of which will, in turn, be intentionally directed to the values for which the organisation purports to stand). One high-profile example of reputational damage, for example, concerned the exposure of labour exploitation practices in the supply chain for Oxfam's 'Make Poverty History' wristbands.
- The need to source inputs for a very wide range of activities, some of which pose significant logistical challenges (eg foreign aid and development work, disaster relief and so on).
- The need to act as retail or merchandise buyers, if goods are resold to raise funds. Procurement officers will therefore have to source goods of a quality, variety and distinctiveness which will appeal to consumers, at a price which allows them to make a significant 'surplus' on the sale. At the same time, there will often be ethical issues involved in dealing fairly with suppliers, and providing suppliers with a fair price for their goods (especially if, like Oxfam for example, the organisation specifically obtains goods from developing countries and small rural suppliers, as part of their charitable activity).
- The need for differentiation (eg via best practice sustainable procurement policies, or distinctive merchandise for re-sale to raise funds) in order to compete for attention, volunteers and funding
- Limited resources. Some third-sector organisations (such as the International Red Cross) have very large procurement budgets. However, many have limited funds, and are anxious to devote as much as possible of their funding to the work for which they were formed: there is therefore a strong emphasis on cost control.

- The need for economic sustainability. The term 'non-profit' or 'not-for-profit' should not be interpreted as implying a disregard for commercial disciplines. On the contrary, such disciplines may be more important than in the private commercial sector, because of the scarcity of funds; pressure to devote as much as possible of their income to beneficiaries; or expenditure limits set by funding authorities (eg grant providers) or trustees. It is worth noting, too, that NFP organisations can enjoy a 'surplus' of income over expenditure, even if it is not described as a 'profit'. Procurement professionals therefore have a key role to play.
- The need for transparency, accountability and stewardship in the management of funds – and resulting oversight and regulation: as discussed earlier.

6 Production and service organisations

6.1 The outputs of an organisation may be either goods (tangible products) or services or a mix of the two. 'Outputs' here refers to what is 'produced' by the organisation. In the case of a manufacturing company, the outputs would be tangible products that the organisation has created and then sells to its customers. In the case of an accountancy firm, say, the output would be a service carried out for a client – perhaps preparation of a tax return or similar.

6.2 Products are tangible, which means that they have a physical presence (unlike services which have no physical presence). The essence of services is that they do not result in the ownership of anything.

Table 1.3 *Characteristics of goods and services*

GOODS	SERVICES
Tangible	Intangible
Can be inventoried	Cannot be inventoried
Little customer contact	Extensive customer contact
Standard customer contact	Flexible customer contact
Long lead times	Short lead times
Capital intensive	Labour intensive
Quality easy to assess	Quality very difficult to assess

6.3 The proportions of goods and services in the mix will vary from industry to industry. Here are some examples (with percentages included for illustration only).

Table 1.4 *The mix of goods and services in different industries*

OPERATION	GOODS	SERVICES
Mining	95%	5%
Vending machines	95%	5%
Low-cost consumable goods	80%	20%
Home computers	75%	25%
Fast-food operation	60%	40%
High-quality restaurant meal	30%	70%
Car breakdown service	25%	75%
Local authority	25%	75%
Teaching	5%	95%

6.4 This analysis demonstrates that most operations produce a mix of goods and services.

6.5 With mining the purpose is to extract raw materials. Little emphasis is placed on the delivery of support services with the exception of transportation to a port or for refinement.

6.6 A fast-food restaurant offers a mix of a limited product range with a standardised approach to service. A more upmarket restaurant provides better facilities and specialised advice. A local authority provides goods in terms of refuse collection, street cleaning etc, but concentrates more on offering a range of support services that meet the needs of the community.

6.7 We are seeing major changes in two key areas that affect the goods-service mix.

- **Customer service requirements**. Customers are becoming more demanding and require better and consistently high levels of customer service. One approach is to use this to the supplier's benefit and 'add value' to the customer experience. Delivery in 24 hours, late product customisation, 'delighting' the customer with unexpected upgrades and improvements at no extra cost, are all examples. The reward can be better customer relationships and retention, leading to an improvement in the operation overall.
- **The impact of information technology**. Information and communication technologies can allow for the provision and standardisation of services in a way that can be easily understood by customers. A well designed website can provide company information, product information and purchase information together with a secure method of purchase and detail on subsequent delivery.

Contrasting services and products

6.8 Services have been defined by marketing guru Philip Kotler as: 'any activity of benefit that one party can offer to another that is essentially intangible and does not result in the ownership of anything. Its production may or may not be tied to a physical product'.

6.9 Carla S Lallatin categorises the services most commonly used by organisations as seen in Figure 1.1.

Figure 1.1 *Lallatin's categorisation of services*

TYPES OF SERVICES				
Personal	**Professional**	**Support**	**Personnel**	**Construction**
Technical editing *Translation* *Appraisals*	*Management and other consultants* *Legal services* *Medical services* *Insurance services*	*Administrative* *Financial* *Information management* *Procurement and logistics services* *Waste management*	*Recruitment and selection* *Training and development* *Welfare services*	*Building repair* *Alteration* *Restoration* *Maintenance services*

6.10 Marketers say that services have the following characteristics that distinguish them from tangible products.

- **Intangibility** refers to the lack of substance that is involved in service delivery. Unlike goods there are no physical aspects, no taste, no feel etc. This can inhibit the choice of a customer to use a service, as they are not sure what they will receive.

- **Inseparability**. A service often cannot be separated from the provider of the service. The creation or the performance of the service often occurs at the same instant that a full or partial consumption of it occurs. Goods must be produced, then sold, then consumed (in that order). Services are only a promise at the time they are sold; most services are sold and then are produced and consumed simultaneously (eg a haircut or a visit to the dentist).
- **Variability**. Many services face a problem of maintaining consistency in the standard of output. Variability of quality in delivery is inevitable because of the number of factors that can influence it. It may prove difficult or impossible either to attain precise standardisation of the service offered or to influence or control perceptions of what is good or bad customer service.
- **Perishability**. Services cannot be stored. Seats at a concert, provision of a lecture, services of a dentist consist of their availability for periods of time. Perishability presents specific marketing problems. Meeting customer needs in these operations depends on staff being available as and when they are needed. This must be balanced against the need for a firm to minimise unnecessary expenditure on staff wages. Anticipating and responding to levels of demand is a key planning priority.
- **Ownership**. Services differ fundamentally from goods in that purchase does not result in a transfer of property. The purchase of a service only confers on the customer access to or rights to use a facility – not ownership. This may lower the customer's perception of the service's value.

6.11 Mirroring this from the purchasing viewpoint, Baily, Farmer, Jessop and Jones in *Purchasing Principles and Management* refer to the following distinctive characteristics of services.

- **Impracticability of storage**. This can give rise to scheduling problems, and the effect of this is that the purchase of services is typically the subject of detailed forward planning between buyer and supplier. Of course, the difficulty does not apply to all services: Baily *et al* cite cleaning services, which are usually not time-critical, and insurance, which is usually provided continuously in return for an annual premium.
- **Lack of inspectability**. A service cannot be measured, weighed or chemically analysed to check compliance with specification. Indeed the whole issue of specifying service levels is very difficult, and many of the problems that commonly arise spring from disagreement between buyer and supplier as to what was agreed.
- **Uncertainties in contractual agreements**. This is another aspect of the specification problem. Baily et al cite the case of an architect who submits a design meeting the criteria of the client in terms of budget, required accommodation etc; and yet the client finds the design unsatisfying on aesthetic grounds. Who, if anyone, is at fault and who pays for the architect's second attempt?
- **Complexity**. The purchase of a tangible asset **sometimes** involves the purchase of a service; for example, if you purchase a large item of machinery, the manufacturer may provide your staff with training on its use. But the converse is **nearly always** true: most service providers will also have to supply tangible product along with the service. For example, a training organisation will invariably provide delegates to its courses with course handouts. This mix of product and service elements adds to the complexity facing the purchaser.

6.12 Services involve a higher degree of customer contact and presentation than with the selling of a product. The physical delivery of a service is less of a problem as the service element is intangible. Consequently some areas take on a more important role than with production-oriented organisations.

- **People**: have a crucial role in providing service. Customer satisfaction can often depend on the person providing the service, because the service is inseparable from the person delivering it. As a result, there is an increased emphasis on staff training and development.
- **Physical evidence**: the ambience surrounding the service being provided. As an example the ambience surrounding a top hotel may serve to convey the nature of the product, reinforce the image of the hotel, create rapport, imply qualities and transmit messages.
- **Process**: this refers to the methods used to provide the service and is directly related to the role of operations management. Procedures for dealing with customers and for supplying the service must be carefully planned and managed so as to reduce variability in quality.

6.13 Among all this discussion of the distinctive nature of services it is easy to forget that there are also essential similarities between services and tangible products.

- Services can be specified and costed.
- Services can be measured and assessed.
- Service suppliers can be rated and assessed.
- Services can be segmented in ways that help purchasers to analyse them.

Chapter summary

- Organisations have been defined as 'social arrangements for the controlled performance of collective goals'.
- Private sector organisations are owned by their investors and aim primarily to make profits. Public sector organisations are owned ultimately by the State and aim primarily to provide defined service levels within agreed budgets.
- Public sector organisations such as government departments and public corporations are financed mainly by taxation.
- The many differences between public sector and private sector organisations do not necessarily lead to major differences in procurement. Increasingly, best procurement practice is transferred across sectors.
- The third sector includes voluntary organisations such as churches and charities, and subscription paid organisations such as clubs and professional bodies.
- A significant factor affecting procurement in the third sector is that they are seen as performing a stewardship function: they are spending funds that derive from other people.
- There are important characteristics that distinguish intangible services from tangible products (such as intangibility, inseparability, variability, perishability, and ownership).

Self-test questions

Numbers in brackets refer to the paragraphs where you can check your answers.

1 Give a definition of an organisation. (1.4)

2 List criteria by which we can classify organisations into different types. (1.7)

3 What is meant by a mixed economy? (1.16)

4 List primary objectives of public sector organisations. (2.6)

5 List differences between public and private sector purchasing. (Table 1.1)

6 List possible objectives pursued by third sector organisations. (4.3)

7 What does it mean to say that NFP organisations perform a stewardship function? (5.1)

8 List types of items procured by NFP organisations. (5.8)

9 List characteristics that distinguish services from tangible products. (6.10, 6.11)

CHAPTER 2

How Organisations Operate

Assessment criteria and indicative content

1.2 Describe how organisations operate

- People, objectives and structure in organisations
- The formal and informal organisation

Section headings

1 People and objectives in organisations
2 Structure in organisations
3 The informal organisation

1 People and objectives in organisations

Objectives in organisations

1.1 Setting effective goals is important for organisational reasons. Goals promote unity of direction, aiding co-ordination and efficient organisation. They reduce overlaps and gaps in activity. They enable limited resources to be intentionally allocated to optimise corporate performance (rather than potentially sub-optimal unit performance). They provide an objective measure against which performance can be measured and accountability maintained. They support flexibility, by focusing on end results rather than inputs (which may change).

1.2 Goal setting is also important, at an individual and team level, for behavioural reasons. Goals enable tasks to be broken down into manageable time-bounded 'chunks', while at the same time giving people a sense of their role and contribution to the whole activity of the organisation. They are important in motivation: people are motivated by the decision that it is worth expending effort to reach desired outcomes (goals), and by feedback information telling them to what extent they have achieved those goals. Goals are, for the same reason, vital in learning and change.

Hierarchy of objectives

1.3 Most writers agree with the idea that there is a hierarchy of objectives in organisations, just as there is a hierarchy of managers. The objectives at the top of the hierarchy are relevant to all aspects and members of the organisation, at a general level. They cascade down to the more specific objectives of business units, groups and individuals. The terms commonly given to the statement of objectives at each stage of this cascade can be pictured as in Figure 2.1

Figure 2.1 *Hierarchy of objectives*

1.4 The **mission** of an organisation is a broad definition of the purpose of the organisation: what business are we in? what are we trying to achieve? The organisation's mission statement is usually a brief statement of the purpose, business areas and key cultural values of the organisation, stated in qualitative rather than quantitative terms. Its purpose is primarily to communicate a sense of meaning and direction to the people inside the organisation, as a guideline for activity.

1.5 Most mission statements are therefore aspirational and customer-focused ('Absolutely, Positively Overnight': Fedex), although some may be competitive ('Beat Coke': Pepsi). They are often broad-brush statements, in order to express the shared values and expectations of different organisational stakeholders.

1.6 Goals and objectives transform the mission or vision into targets or aims which the organisation will pursue. The terms are often used interchangeably, but it may be helpful to think of goals as statements of a desired future state ('where we want to get to'), and objectives as more specific, time-assigned, quantified targets to pursue in order to achieve each goal ('what we need to do to get there').

1.7 Finally, objectives should be flexible. Monitoring and feedback may indicate the need not just to correct or adjust performance in line with objectives, but to adjust the objectives themselves: circumstances or needs may have changed. The longer-ranging the objectives are, in turbulent business environments, the less fixed objectives may have to be, in order to avoid dysfunctional rigidity.

Departmental, team and individual work objectives

1.8 As the hierarchy of planning suggests, objectives may be set at a number of levels. At the corporate level, they spell out the organisation's mission and strategic plans. At the departmental or functional level, they set out the specific targets or key results to be achieved by the function in order to contribute to strategic plans. At the team level, they set out the key results or contribution expected of the team, in order to achieve departmental goals. And at the individual level, they are job-related or role-related: what results are individuals expected to achieve, to what standard, in what key activity areas, in order for all the higher objectives to be achieved?

1.9 You may see these presented to you as one of the following.

- Quantified output or improvement targets (eg increase orders processed by 3% by 5 April; reduce wastage by 5% in the next six months; maintain inventory levels at no more than $9 million)
- Performance standards, whether quantified (eg process 90% of customer orders within 24 hours, the remaining 10% to be acknowledged same day and processed within three working days) or qualitative (eg performance will be up to standard if proposals for new product material specifications are fully supported by relevant data on materials and sources, justified by return-on-investment analysis, and compliant with environmental and ethical policies)
- Projects to be completed (eg report on overseas supplier ethical performance by 30 June; open distribution depot in Mombasa by 15 September). *Armstrong* gives the following example of a project objective which also sets out relevant success criteria: 'Introduce a new stock control system by 30 November to provide more accurate, comprehensive and immediate information on stock and thus enable inventory targets to be achieved without prejudicing production flows or customer service levels.'
- Standing objectives: ongoing, continuous targets or standards which are a consistent part of the job (eg deliveries to be made within three days of receiving an order; ethical guidelines for purchasing to be upheld at all times).

1.10 If an organisation is to achieve its many different objectives, they must be co-ordinated with each other so that they contribute towards the overall goal. **Alignment** (or integration) is the term given to this fitting together of objectives. It needs to happen in two directions.

1.11 **Vertical alignment** is about ensuring that the goal of every activity contributes towards the overall or higher objectives of the business. Objectives for strategic change are designed to reflect the organisation's mission. They are, in turn, expressed as functional objectives – which are, in turn, expressed as unit objectives.

1.12 So, for example, an organisation with a vision for innovation may set objectives for new product development. These will flow down to purchasing objectives (among others) for adding value to materials and quality specifications. Conversely, any change objectives set for a unit or function must be in line with (and justified by their contribution to) overall strategies.

1.13 **Horizontal alignment** is about ensuring that the plans of every unit in an organisation are co-ordinated with those of others, so that they work effectively together – and present a consistent, coherent face to the world. So, for example, purchasing and supply plans must be co-ordinated with the needs of customers (defined by marketing plans), the requirements of operations (defined by operations plans) and the availability of resources (eg through HR and financial planning) and so on. Purchasing's handling of supply chain relationships must not only ensure secure supply and work flow to business processes: it must also reflect the organisation's values about business ethics, partnership and collaboration, and so on.

Setting SMART objectives

1.14 Effective objectives are 'SMART'.

- Specific: precise, clear and well-defined, so people know what they are committing to and accountable for.
- Measurable: related to quantified measures (reduce errors or costs by *x*% over *x* months) or qualitative measures (increase expressed customer satisfaction), so that people can assess their progress and achievement.
- Attainable: achievable, given the time and resources available – even if the aim is to be 'stretching', the objective must be possible.
- Relevant: to the strategic objectives of the business unit and the organisation as a whole.
- Time-bounded: given a defined time-scale over which the objective will be achieved.

1.15 Some versions substitute, or add:

- Stretching: objectives must be challenging enough to motivate people and bring learning, development and improvement
- Rewarded: attainment of the objectives is linked to positive rewards of some kind
- Reviewed: plans should include a methodology and time-scales for monitoring and reviewing progress and results.

1.16 Some prefer SMARTER, adding:

- ***E**valuated*: The objective must have been assessed as worth pursuing, given the investment in time or effort it will require: this may involve some form of cost-benefit analysis
- ***R**esponsible*: The objective must take into account potential impacts on key stakeholders, in the light of the unit's (and organisation's) ethical responsibilities towards them.

2 Structure in organisations

2.1 *Laurie Mullins* defines organisation structure as 'the pattern of relationships among positions in the organisation and among members of the organisation. Structure makes possible the application of the process of management and creates a framework of order and command through which the activities of the organisation can be planned, organised, directed and controlled'. *Henry Mintzberg* defines an organisation's structure as: 'the sum total of the ways in which it divides its labour into distinct tasks and then achieves co-ordination among them'.

2.2 Formal organisation structure or design therefore consists of a framework whose purpose is as follows.

- To define work roles and relationships, so that areas and flows of authority and responsibility are clearly established
- To define work tasks and responsibilities, grouping and allocating them to suitable individuals and groups
- To channel information flows efficiently through the organisation
- To co-ordinate goals and activities of different units, so that organisational goals can be efficiently achieved (ie without duplication of effort)
- To control the flow of work, information and resources, through planning, monitoring and other systems
- To support flexible working and adaptability to changing internal and external demands
- To encourage and support the commitment, involvement and satisfaction of the people who

work for the organisation, by offering opportunities for participation, challenge, interest, responsibility, teamworking and so on
- To support and improve the efficiency and effectiveness of the organisation's performance through all of the above

2.3 *Peter Drucker* argued that: 'good organisation structure does not by itself produce good performance. But a poor organisation structure makes good performance impossible, no matter how good the individual managers may be. To improve organisation structure ... will therefore always improve performance.'

2.4 Note, however, that an effective organisation structure is one that both facilitates organisational effectiveness and efficiency in the long term (taking into account the need for change) *and* meets the needs of the people working within it.

2.5 Signs that a structure may be **ineffective** therefore include problems such as the following.

- Slow decision or response times, due to the need to refer decisions via overly lengthy formal communication channels
- Inter-departmental conflicts, due to ambiguities or overlaps of responsibility
- Excessive layers of management (often middle management), which slows communication, increases overheads and often requires work creation to justify the positions
- Lack of co-ordination between units, seen in customer complaints, production bottlenecks, inconsistent communications, and the creation of special co-ordinating mechanisms (liaison officers, committees etc)
- High labour turnover among skilled junior staff, suggesting lack of development opportunities
- Lack of identifiable accountabilities for key tasks.

What shapes an organisation's structure?

2.6 There are many influences on organisation structure. There are certain internal principles and dynamics of organisation: how far power and authority are held at the top (centralised) or given to lower levels (decentralised); the span of control (the number of subordinates that can be supervised by any one superior); the division of labour; the grouping of people into working units; the need for communication channels, and so on. These determine some elements of structure, to an extent, according to internal logic.

2.7 A number of variables may influence structural choices and organisational development.

- The **strategic objectives** or **mission** of the organisation, and how these are broken down to define and guide the work of sub-units. Diversified organisations, for example, may require more decentralised structures. (A diversified organisation is one that provides numerous, varied products and/or services.)
- The **task** or 'business' of the organisation, which will determine which line or task functions are required (development, production, marketing, finance) and which support or staff functions (HR, planning, quality control, maintenance).
- The **technology** of the task may necessitate certain forms of organisation to maximise its efficiency and the needs of people.
- The **size** of the organisation. As it gets larger, its structure will get more complex: specialisation, subdivision and formalisation are required in order to control and co-ordinate performance (typically leading to bureaucratic structures in large organisations).
- **Geographical dispersion** may require federalised structures to take into account relevant

factors at local, regional, national, international or global levels of operation. (A federalised structure means that there may be many local business units, each with a measure of independence, but with a 'head office' exercising overall control. The political structure of the USA is an example of a federalised structure.)

- The **environment** of the organisation. Factors (and especially changes) in the legal, commercial, technical and social environment represent demands and constraints on organisational activity, and opportunities and threats to which organisation structure must adapt. As one example, information and communication technology (ICT) has enabled organisations to adopt looser, more network-style units or 'virtual teams'.
- The **culture and management** style of the organisation: eg the willingness of management to delegate authority and adopt more fluid facilitate-and-empower roles; organisational values about teamworking, formality, flexibility and so on.

People in organisations

2.8 People pursue objectives, both their own and the organisation's, within the structure of the organisation. In doing so, they have a degree of fit with the organisation and commitment to it. They also have defined roles and responsibilities, as well as a defined place within the organisational hierarchy.

2.9 **Span of control** is one of the main internal principles of organisation. Span of control (also called 'span of management') is the number of subordinates responsible to any one superior, and is used for all levels in a management hierarchy. If three people report directly to a manager, the span of control is three: Figure 2.2.

Figure 2.2 *Span of control (3)*

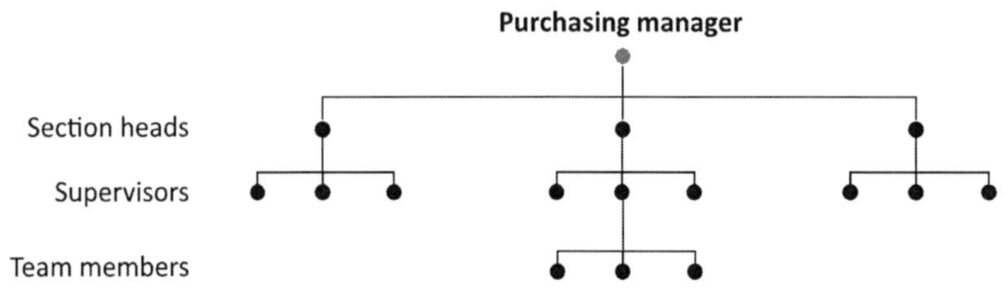

2.10 Classical theorists such as Henri Fayol argued that the span of control should be restricted (between three and six) because while there needs to be managerial control over activities at every level of the organisation, there are also physical and mental limitations to a manager's ability to keep track of people, relationships and activities at the level of detail required.

2.11 If span of control is too wide, too much of the manager's time will be taken up with routine problems and supervision, leaving less time for higher management functions. Even so, people may not get the supervision or communication they require, because the manager is 'spread too thin'. Arguments for a **narrow** span of control include:

- Tighter control of activities
- Better communication and co-ordination
- More efficient use of managerial time and costs (through less supervisory activity)
- Reduced need for managers to delegate (if this is considered undesirable, eg where team members lack capability to take on responsibility)

- More efficient and satisfying teamwork, if units are organised as small groups or project teams.

2.12 If the span of control is too narrow, however, the manager may over-supervise the work of subordinates and may feel no pressure to delegate at all. The arguments for a **wide** span of control therefore include:

- More efficient use of managerial time and costs (through delegation)
- More discretion for subordinates, potentially contributing to job satisfaction, organisational flexibility and innovation.

2.13 The appropriate span will depend on various factors.

- The capabilities of the manager to plan, organise, co-ordinate and control activities, resources and people, and to manage his own time effectively
- The nature of the manager's workload, which will influence the amount of supervisory activity he will be able to handle effectively
- The capabilities of the subordinates. The more competent, trustworthy and motivated subordinates are, the easier it is to control a wider span. They may also have higher expectations in regard to delegation.
- The nature and technology of the task. A wide span is possible where the task is routine, repetitive or automated. Greater managerial input – and therefore a narrower span of control – may be required where there are more complex, interlocking tasks; where demands and technologies are constantly changing; or where there are high risks attached to errors.
- The dynamics of teamworking. If subordinates are able to communicate freely between themselves, and support each other in solving work tasks, then less supervision is required and there may be a wider span of control.
- The co-ordinatory mechanisms of the organisation. If subordinates are geographically dispersed, or the communication systems of the organisation are inadequate, the span will need to be narrower. ICT has widened spans of control, enabling managers to co-ordinate data-sharing and activities more efficiently.

Centralisation and decentralisation of authority

2.14 The terms **centralisation** and **decentralisation** are used to refer to:

- The extent to which decision-making authority is kept close to the centre (or top) of the firm: ie the level of the hierarchy at which decisions are taken – and the extent of delegation.
- The extent to which related tasks and resources are gathered under a single functional authority or location: eg whether there is a separate purchasing function, or whether purchasing is carried out by relevant line departments.

2.15 Absolute decentralisation is not possible because any delegated authority can derive only from the top, and activities must conform to the policies decided at a higher level. But then, absolute centralisation of authority is not practical except in very small concerns, because the sheer volume of decisions would overwhelm those at the top.

2.16 The choice of organisation structure will depend to a certain extent on the preferences of the organisation's top management, but equally important is the size of the organisation and the scale of its activities. Thus the small business structure is likely to be centralised, and the divisional structure is likely to be decentralised.

3 The informal organisation

3.1 As social arrangements, organisations are collections of individuals who experience common membership, occupy different roles, and share common goals – but also have goals and interests of their own. Organisations are, moreover, accountable in various ways to their owners and other interested parties (or 'stakeholders') for the achievement of their stated objectives and the use of their human, financial and material resources. These twin pressures of diversity and accountability create the need to control performance.

3.2 The need for controlled performance leads in turn to features of business organisations such as: a deliberately ordered environment; the allocation of tasks (division of labour); the setting of standards and targets (planning); and the measurement of results against them (control). This implies a structure of power and responsibility relationships (whereby some individuals determine and/or oversee the work of others) and a structure of communication channels (through which instructions, reports and feedback information flow).

3.3 All these elements are features of the **formal organisation structure**. In the next chapter we will look at examples of formal organisation structures (such as functional structures, geographical structures etc).

Informal organisation

3.4 Within – or underneath – every formal organisation, there is a complex informal organisation.

3.5 Formal organisation has a well-defined, fixed structure of task-focused roles and relationships which remains stable regardless of changes of membership. Informal organisation, in contrast, is a loosely structured, spontaneous, fluctuating network of interpersonal relationships.

3.6 When people work together, they establish:

- **Social networks and groups**, the boundaries of units established by the formal organisation.
- **Informal ways of getting things done**, often different from the formal rules and procedures of the organisation.
- **Informal communication networks**, often bypassing formal communication channels. This is sometimes called the 'grapevine' or 'bush telegraph'.
- **Informal authority structures**, often different from the formal position-based scalar chain of command. Non-managerial individuals may have informal influence over their colleagues (and even over their superiors).

3.7 These informal structures may support the objectives of the formal organisation. However, there is also potential for the informal organisation to work against the objectives of the formal organisation. When employees are dissatisfied with aspects of the formal organisation, they are likely to rely more heavily on the informal organisation for information, satisfying relationships and less frustrating ways of getting things done.

3.8 Formal communication systems, in particular, benefit from the support of a positive informal network – and suffer from undermining by a negative informal network.

Networks and the virtual organisation

3.9 The term 'network organisation' refers to a looser, dynamic, more informal affiliation of autonomous and broadly equal organisations, who exchange information and pursue ongoing (typically long-term) relationships for mutual benefit.

3.10 There are no direct contractual or financial obligations (eg investment by one company in another) shaping these relationships. They are purely based on collaboration, communication, trust and mutual advantage.

3.11 A special form of the network concept is the virtual organisation, where companies (or units of a single company) collaborate, co-ordinate their activities and share data, using information communications technology (ICT) as their main – or only – point of contact.

3.12 Operations can be geographically dispersed, global expertise drawn on, functions outsourced and 24-hour/seven-day communication maintained – while operating (to all intents and purposes) as a single organisational entity. Tasks are typically fragmented, performed by widely dispersed individuals, but integrated by communication and data-sharing, eg via the internet – online databases, interactive websites, email contact, and web-conferencing, tele-conferencing and video-conferencing. Web retailer Amazon.com is perhaps the best known virtual organisation.

3.13 The virtual organisation model is gaining popularity as an organisational structure for several reasons.

- Virtual organisations are supported by ongoing developments in ICT which allow data-sharing and synchronisation, interactive communication and virtual meetings (eg by webcast), across barriers of time and geographical distance.
- They allow a high degree of flexibility (numerical, temporal and functional). Membership is diverse and structurally fluid enough to respond flexibly to equally diverse and changing customer and client requirements.
- They enable information and other resources to be mobilised efficiently in widely dispersed regions and specialist sectors, while allowing central control, pooled information and consistency of service and image where required.
- They offer cost savings in areas such as employment (no redundancy obligations, benefits), overheads and logistics, owing to the physical dispersal of (and loose contractual relationship with) members.
- They exploit an increasingly knowledge-based economy, where the prime commodities are knowledge, information and expertise.
- They exploit international markets, as they enable members to take advantage of local knowledge, native language speakers, indigenous trading partnerships, etc.

Chapter summary

- There is a hierarchy of organisational objectives: mission; goals; objectives; strategy; tactics; operational plans.
- Objectives must be aligned both vertically (contributing to higher objectives) and horizontally (co-ordinated with other functions in the organisation).
- Effective objectives are SMART: specific; measurable; attainable; relevant; time-bounded.
- Formal organisation structure is 'the pattern of relationships among positions in the organisation and among members of the organisation'.
- Span of control is the number of subordinates responsible to any one superior. Arguments can be made for either a wide span of control or a narrow span of control.
- Informal organisation is a loosely structured, spontaneous, fluctuating network of interpersonal relationships.
- In a virtual organisation companies, departments or individuals collaborate, co-ordinate their activities and share data using ICT as their only means of contact.

Self-test questions

Numbers in brackets refer to the paragraphs where you can check your answers.

1 Sketch a hierarchy of organisational objectives. (Figure 2.1)

2 Explain what is meant by vertical and horizontal alignment of organisational objectives. (1.11, 1.13)

3 What is meant by SMART and SMARTER objectives? (1.14, 1.16)

4 List purposes of formal organisation structure. (2.2)

5 List signs that an organisation structure is ineffective. (2.5)

6 Give arguments for (a) a narrow span of control and (b) a wide span of control. (2.11, 2.12)

7 What is meant by centralisation and decentralisation of authority? (2.14)

8 What is meant by the informal organisation? (3.6, 3.7)

9 Define a network organisation. (3.9)

10 List features of virtual organisations. (3.11)

CHAPTER 3

Key Operating Functions Within Organisations

Assessment criteria and indicative content

1.2 Describe how organisations operate

- The formal and informal organisation

1.3 Identify the main operating functions within organisations

- Differentiation and integration in organisations
- Typical functions in organisations such as production, operations, marketing and sales, customer support, human resources, personnel, finance, IT, and technical functions
- Differentiating procurement and supply

Section headings

1 Differentiation and integration in organisations
2 Typical functions in organisations
3 The procurement and supply function

1 Differentiation and integration in organisations

The work of Lawrence and Lorsch

1.1 An organisation must find ways of dividing up the various tasks it must achieve in order to fulfil its main purposes without losing overall co-ordination and integration.

1.2 Differentiation refers to 'dividing up' in organisations. As an organisation becomes more complex, one person can no longer carry out all the work. There is a need to divide up tasks among people, and specialised roles develop. For example, as a small-scale manufacturer develops, the work of purchasing components becomes a job in its own right. As the company grows so does the need for better and more specialised purchasing and so on.

1.3 As organisations grow, it becomes harder for people in different specialised sections to keep in contact with one another. This creates a need for an internal process where people from different business areas can co-ordinate their efforts. The need can be met by meetings, cross-functional working groups etc. This activity – referred to as integration – adds another layer of complexity to the organisation.

1.4 This theme of 'differentiation and integration' was developed by Lawrence and Lorsch (1967). Their examples are based on the chemical industry, but similar issues arise in all kinds of organisations. They found that differences in the structures of successful companies in the food and plastics industries were related to the amount of differentiation required by the environments in which they operated. They posed the question: why do people seek to build organisations? The answer they reached was that organisations enable people to find better solutions to the challenges posed by their environment.

1.5 This answer led them to three conclusions about organisational behaviour.

- People (not organisations) have purposes or goals.
- People have to come together to co-ordinate their different activities and thus create an organisation.
- The effectiveness of an organisation depends on how well people's needs are satisfied by their planned transactions with their particular environment.

1.6 As they grow, organisations develop specialised units to deal with segments of their external environment. This differentiation of function and task within an organisation will be matched by different priorities, values and structures in the different units. These differentiated tasks and sections need to connect with one another. This is the required integration and it too is affected by the nature of the external conditions.

1.7 Lawrence and Lorsch found that the firms they studied differentiated their functions into sub-units which dealt with a market environment (the task of sales), a techno-economic environment (the task of manufacturing) and a scientific environment (the task of research and development). The greater the degree of uncertainty within each sub-environment and the greater the diversity between them, the greater was the need of the firms to differentiate between their sub-units in order to be effective in each sub-environment.

1.8 Greater differentiation may lead to increased interdepartmental conflict as the specialist groups develop their own ways of dealing with their particular environment. These differences may involve fundamental ways of thinking and behaving. Management tools such as the mission statement are designed to ensure that the organisation and everyone in it is focusing in the same direction.

1.9 The impact of technology may be reducing differentiation. Purchasing is now closer to logistics than it used to be, and is also more involved in marketing. As these changes gradually occur differentiation may reduce and a more integrated company model may develop.

1.10 Although people often imagine that their organisation would be more effective if only everyone else thought as they did, Lawrence and Lorsch's analysis suggests that quite the opposite is true. If everyone thought as the production staff do (or the administrators, or the sales people), organisations would be thoroughly ineffective. Organisations need to incorporate very different perspectives and concerns even if this causes integration problems.

Common organisational structures

1.11 This issue of differentiation and integration is a key factor in shaping organisational structure. In a very small company, people can simply share the tasks between them according to their skills. Once an organisation grows beyond a certain size, however, systematic specialisation is required. This typically involves the grouping together and allocation of specific aspects of the work to different departments. This can be done on the basis of criteria such as:

- Functional specialisation

- Geographical area or territory
- Product, brand or customer.

1.12 We will look at each of these in turn.

Functional organisation

1.13 In a functional structure, tasks are grouped together according to the common nature or focus of the task: production, sales and marketing, accounting and finance, purchasing and so on. An example of a functionally structured organisation is shown in Figure 3.1.

Figure 3.1 *Functional organisation*

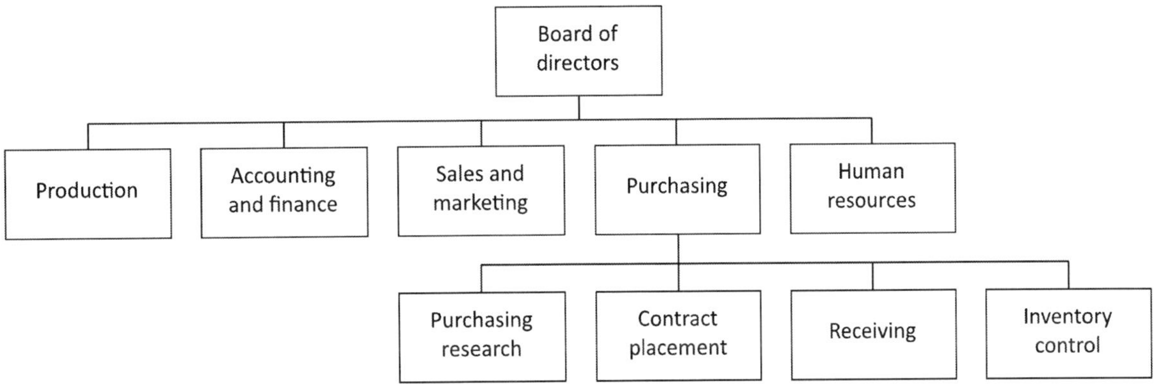

Geographical organisation

1.14 In a geographical structure, tasks are grouped together according to the region in which the activity takes place, or within which target markets or market segments are located. Multi-site organisations (eg a purchasing function organised by plant) and sales departments (with allocated 'territories') are often organised this way. An example of a geographically-structured organisation is shown in Figure 3.2.

Figure 3.2 *Geographical organisation*

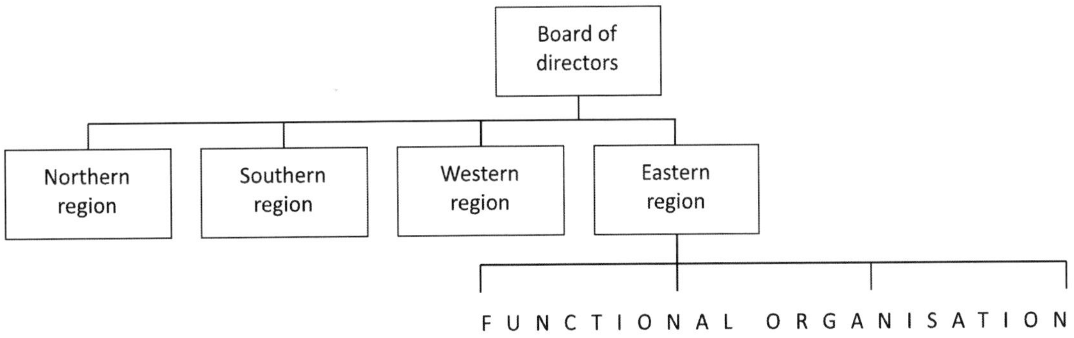

Product, brand or customer organisation

1.15 In a product structure, tasks are grouped together according to the product, product line, customer or brand they relate to. Companies with distinct brands (such as Coca Cola or Persil) often organise in this way, so that there is specialisation of brand marketing and identity – and separate brand accountabilities. Similarly, companies with key customer types, such as publishers (for example bookshops, educational institutions, libraries) may group together tasks in this way. In purchasing, the equivalent may be organisation by items purchased: Figure 3.3.

Figure 3.3 *Product, brand or customer organisation*

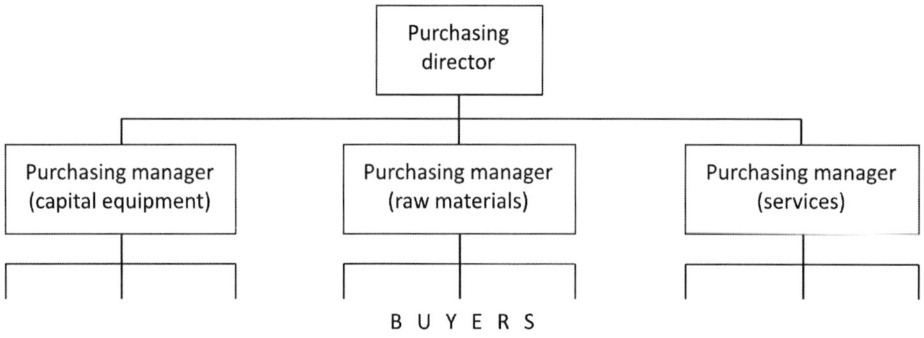

Divisionalisation

1.16 Divisionalisation is the division of the organisation into more or less independent strategic business units (SBUs), as the business diversifies into new areas. Divisions may be:

- **Profit or investment centres within a company**. Strategic planning and other support activities (such as finance, HR, research and development and perhaps purchasing) are undertaken at a central board or 'head office' level. Divisions may be based on function (retail division, manufacturing division), product (hardware division, software division) or region (Asian-Pacific division, European division). Each division may then be organised in an appropriate way: see Figure 3.4.
- **Subsidiary companies grouped under a holding company**. When businesses grow through acquisition, or require a high degree of differentiation in product or regional divisions, they may form a group of independent public or private companies, owned or controlled by a holding company.

Figure 3.4 *Divisional structure*

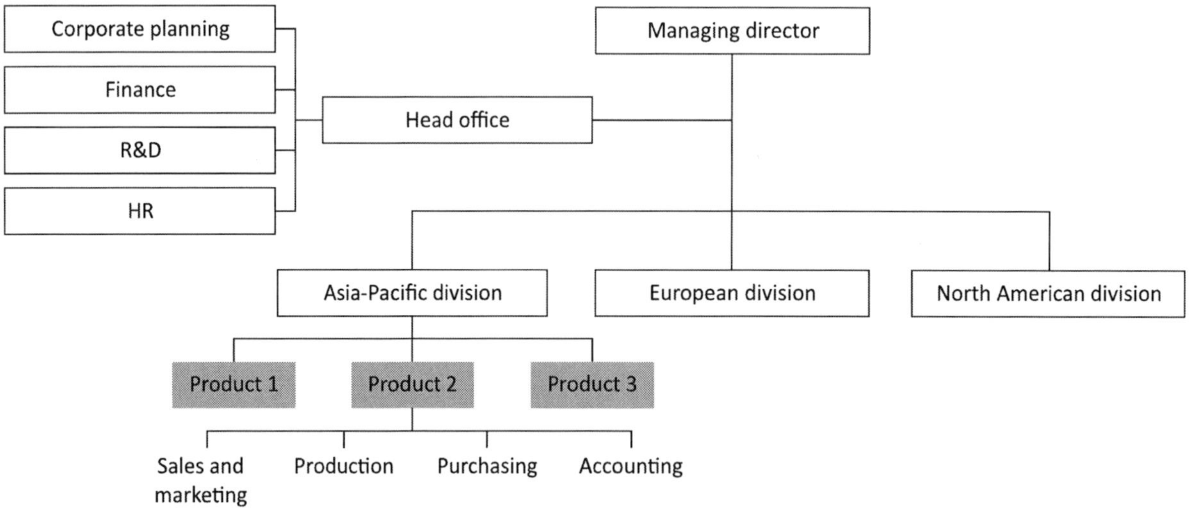

Matrix structures

1.17 The 'matrix' structure emerged at American aerospace company Lockheed in the 1950s, when its customer (the US government) became frustrated at dealing separately with a number of functional specialists when negotiating defence contracts. The concept of the 'project co-ordinator' or 'customer account manager' was born.

1.18 The essence of matrix structure is dual authority: staff in different functions or regions are responsible both to their departmental managers, in regard to the activities of the department, and to a product, project or account manager, in regard to the activities of the department related to the given product, project or account.

1.19 The matrix can be illustrated as follows, in the case of an advertising agency: Figure 3.5.

Figure 3.5 *Matrix organisation*

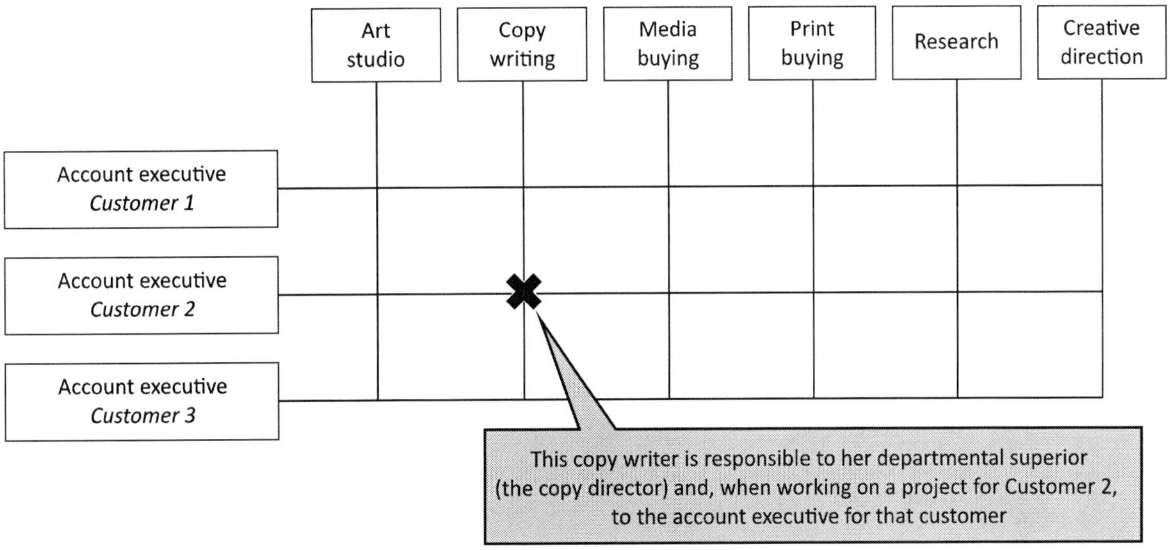

Advantages and disadvantages of different structural forms

1.20 The advantages and disadvantages of the various forms of organisation are summarised in Table 3.1.

Table 3.1 *Different structural forms*

ORGANISATION	ADVANTAGES	DISADVANTAGES
Functional	• Pools and focuses specialised skills and knowledge • Share specialised technology and equipment for efficiency • Facilitates the recruitment, training and management of specialist staff • Avoids duplicating functions within area or product departments: enables economies of scale	• Focuses on inputs and processes rather than outputs and customers (necessary for customer satisfaction) • Creates vertical barriers to cross-disciplinary communication (necessary to flexibility and co-ordination)
Geographical	• Decision-making at the interface between organisation and local stakeholders (with distinctive needs) • Cost-effective (because shorter) lines of supply and communication to local markets or plants	• Duplication of functional activities • Loss of standardisation, due to local differences
Product, brand or customer	• Clearer accountability for the profitability of different products, brands and customer groups • Specialisation of production and marketing expertise • Co-ordination of different functions by product managers	• Increased managerial complexity and overhead costs • Possible fragmentation of objectives and markets
Divisionalisation	• Clear accountability for each division as a profit or investment unit • Sensitivity demands and opportunities specific to regions or products • Efficiencies and economies of scale available from centralised functions • Co-ordination available from centralised strategic planning and control	• Potential fragmentation of overall objectives and markets • Potential conflict between central management and divisional specialists • Potential competition between divisions for centrally-allocated resources • Units may not be large enough to support managerial overheads
Matrix structures	• Combines functional efficiency with product or project accountability • Fosters interdisciplinary co-operation in pursuit of project goals • Develops tolerance of flexibility and ambiguity: improved change, learning • Focuses all functions on customer satisfaction and results: more satisfying • Brings conflicts of authority into the open	• Potential competition or conflict between dual managers • Potential stress on staff 'caught' between competing or conflicting demands • Potential inefficiency of ambiguous priorities and switching between tasks • More complex (potentially slower) decision-making processes • Costs of added management layer, meetings and so on

Hybrid structures

1.21 'Hybrid' simply means 'crossed' or 'mixed'. As you may have noticed from the various organisation charts shown above, businesses generally combine a variety of organisational forms. For example, they may be organised by region or product at divisional level, with functional departments within each division. Hybrid structures allow the advantages of each form of organisation to be leveraged in appropriate ways: brand identity to be reinforced by a product division, for example, with regional knowledge to be capitalised on by its sales departments and economies of scale to be gained by a specialised purchasing department.

2 Typical functions in organisations

Production

2.1 Production is the functional area responsible for turning inputs into finished outputs through a series of production processes. The Production Manager is responsible for making sure that raw materials are provided and made into finished goods effectively. Their responsibilities include ensuring that work is carried out smoothly with no bottlenecks, and supervision of procedures for making work more efficient and more enjoyable.

2.2 **Production** will set standards and targets for each section of the production process. The quantity and quality of products coming off a production line will be closely monitored. In businesses focusing on lean production (ie minimising wasted resources), quality will be monitored by all employees at every stage of production, rather than at the end (as is the case for businesses using a quality control approach).

2.3 A key aspect of modern production is ensuring quality. The term quality means, 'fitness for purpose'. In other words, a product, process or service should do exactly what is expected of it.

2.4 The department will organise, manage and monitor the production or assembly of goods (or services). This will include all maintenance work involved in the production process and other necessary repairs.

2.5 Working closely with the warehouse, purchasing, design and development functions, production produces the goods that keep the business in operation.

Operations

2.6 An operations department (sometimes called a back office function) typically attends to those administrative, logistical, and other duties necessary for an organisation's day-to-day functioning. Depending on the nature of the organisation, an operations department may be responsible for a diverse range of responsibilities.

2.7 Operations departments exist in businesses and other organisations in every segment of the economy, including – but not limited to – such segments as the financial services industry, including banks and brokerages, as well as academia, manufacturing, non-profit organisations, and the armed forces.

2.8 Operations departments and production departments can fulfil the same function in manufacture. For example, in a chemical company the operations department is the department that refines and processes the chemicals.

Marketing and sales

2.9 The role of this department is to understand the 'needs and wants' of customers. The focus on 'customer service levels' is a measure of the importance of customers throughout all organisations and increasingly so in today's competitive global market.

2.10 Marketing and sales both are important activities for every organisation. Marketing is a broader term than sales. It includes such activities as public relations, branding, advertising, and sales. In other words, sales is one part or activity of the marketing function.

2.11 Marketing is concerned with identifying and then satisfying the needs of customers and potential customers. Sales is concerned with persuading customers that the company's products and services are what they need.

2.12 There is one more important difference between marketing and sales and that is the focus. Marketing is concerned with educating and creating awareness of the product or service in the market. Sales, as the term suggests, is concerned with converting such awareness into actual orders.

2.13 Marketing will often seek flexibility in the production process so that they can better satisfy customer needs. This may be met by adopting a flexible manufacturing system that can adapt to late changes and modifications or by designing a system that permits **late customisation**. Late customisation refers to the system of production in which most manufacturing is done in advance, but the final touches are only completed when a customer order is received. An often quoted example of this is the way that Dell Computers operate.

Customer support

2.14 Customer support is a range of customer services used to assist customers in making cost effective and correct use of a product. It can encompass assistance in planning, installation, training, trouble shooting, maintenance, upgrading, and disposal of a product.

2.15 The customer support role in a company is to respond to enquiries and complaints from customers. Customer support is an important part of the fulfilment function, ensuring that customers will buy again and/or continue to be good customers.

2.16 Customer service is the provision of a service to customers before, during and after a purchase. According to Turban et al (2002) 'Customer service is a series of activities designed to enhance the level of customer satisfaction – that is, the feeling that a product or service has met the customer's expectation'.

2.17 Customer support can be viewed as the support mechanisms in place to ensure that any enquiries a customer has about a product can be answered and clarified. The customer support role is often linked with customer service which takes customer support further and tries to ensure that all the customer needs are met, and that the customer will return and buy again.

Human resource management/personnel

2.18 Human resource managers are responsible for ensuring that the workforce is meeting the needs of the organisation now and in the future.

2.19 Production is often a labour intensive function and requires that the human resource team understand the production process and the human resource needs of the operation. Production often requires a flexible workforce to meet fluctuating demand and requires that the workforce and associated employment contracts are designed in such a way as to meet this demand.

2.20 Operational changes will often lead to new skills being required that may be met by training programmes or additional recruitment and/or redundancies. These issues require the specialist input that the human resource function can bring.

Finance

2.21 The role of the finance department is to evaluate the effectiveness of any changes proposed or made from a financial perspective.

2.22 Finance will require a business case to be presented and accepted before committing to expenditure. Capital expenditure, in particular, will be carefully scrutinised and options such as lower-cost alternatives and outsourcing evaluated. Purchase options such as leasing, hiring or hire purchase will also be evaluated as options to purchase.

2.23 Finance have an interest in manufacturing costs as these will often represent a substantial amount of organisational expenditure. Systems such as MRPII (manufacturing resources planning) allow for detailed costing of manufacturing runs by apportioning costs for labour, machinery and overheads to individual jobs. The expenditure made by production forms an ongoing interface between finance and operations as reduction of costs is a common goal of both functions.

IT and engineering

2.24 Other key functions of the organisation require consideration. The IT department's importance reflects the development stage of the operations role. Modern production operations are highly computer dependent and as such will have an ongoing dialogue with IT services.

2.25 An integrated approach to IT where systems carry information on suppliers, deliveries and stock management, is important in regard to the input stage of the transformation process. The availability of real time information aids the operations role particularly when planning and scheduling production.

2.26 Engineering staff bring specialist skills to an organisation. Their ideas will often result in development through to production. The involvement in cross-functional teamwork with engineering is important as operations will take over responsibility for manufacture if the concept is developed.

Technical functions

2.27 Technical support refers to the range of services that enterprises use to provide assistance to users of technology products such as mobile phones, televisions, computers, software products or other electronic or mechanical goods. In general, technical support services attempt to help the user solve specific problems with a product as opposed to providing training, customisation, or other support services.

2.28 Most technology companies offer technical support for the products they sell, either free of charge or for a fee. Technical support may be delivered over the telephone or online. Online support may be provided by email or through a website.

2.29 Larger organisations frequently have internal technical support available to their staff for computer related problems. The internet is also a good source for freely available technical support, where experienced users may provide advice and assistance with problems. In addition, some fee-based service companies charge for premium technical support services.

3 The procurement and supply function

The historical development of procurement and supply

3.1 Purchasing will achieve its maximum contribution to organisational goals only if its status in the organisation is sufficiently recognised. If the function is still seen primarily as providing administrative and clerical services, the opportunity to influence organisational achievement and delight internal customers will be limited.

3.2 Historically, the purchasing department has often been regarded as a support function, subordinated to production. This perception has gradually changed. Nowadays it is common in large organisations to find that the head of purchasing either reports directly to a main board director or is himself a director on the main board.

3.3 Lysons identifies three hierarchical levels at which purchasing may operate.

- At the lowest level, purchasing is a routine clerical function. As Lysons states, this may well be the case in a small business, or perhaps in a group situation where centralised policies and procedures leave little scope for initiative at local level.
- As purchasing advances, it may become a middle management function. The head of purchasing, whatever his title, reports to a level well below that of the main board, perhaps to a production director if purchasing is seen as a support service for production. This situation may also apply if purchasing is seen as one element in a materials or logistics management structure.
- At the highest level, the head of purchasing may be a member of senior management, perhaps on the main board of the company or group.

3.4 The progression through these stages may well be driven by growing consciousness of purchasing's effect on profitability. As the proportion of external spending rises relative to internal spending the scope for purchasing to improve bottom line profits increases. Another stimulus is given by the rise in automation, leading to very high levels of investment in capital assets. In this area, the need to 'get it right' dictates that specialist purchasing skills are used.

Differentiating procurement and supply

3.5 The historical development mapped out briefly above is relevant to the term 'procurement and supply'. This term is often used as though it is just a single activity – the work that purchasing professionals carry out every day.

3.6 However, it is more accurate to distinguish between the two halves of the term.

- Procurement (or purchasing) is the process of placing orders and acquiring supplies. In the early days of the profession, buyers did no more than this – they just reacted to requisitions by placing orders with suppliers.
- Supply is the act or process of providing something or making something available, often in response to buyers' or customers' requirements. It involves the transfer or flow of goods, services and information from one party (a supplier) to another (a customer).

Influencing factors

3.7 The published guidance from CIPS *(Harris and Botten)* highlights a number of key factors which influence the design of the purchasing function.

3.8 The **size, nature and role** of the purchasing and supply task in the organisation.

- It may, for example, be transactional, commercial or strategic in orientation (reflected by its expenditure and level of reporting in the organisation).
- It may cover a range of activities, dictating a degree of specialisation: as size and specialisation grows, additional attention may need to be given to mechanisms for control and communication.
- It may be a dedicated function, reporting at the highest level of the organisation – or it may (increasingly rarely, in large organisations) be a subsidiary function reporting through production, finance or commerce.

3.9 **Alignment**. Purchasing accountabilities may be subdivided by: category of purchased items (eg MRO, commodities, vehicles); the product category for which supplies are to be used; the stage of manufacture (eg raw materials, components, finished assemblies); plant location; supplier group; or internal customer group (eg different departments in a local authority).

3.10 The **structure and environment** within which purchasing operates.

- The internal organisation structure: what functions purchasing reports to (and at what level); what mechanisms there are to co-ordinate purchasing activities with those of other functions; who the internal customers of purchasing are; the nature of purchasing's role in relation to them (direct service provider, advisor, regulator); how purchasing competence and contribution is perceived and measured in the organisation; how purchasing reflects the wider organisation structure and culture; and so on.
- The supply market and the organisation's supply base: its size, geographical spread, structure, degree of specialisation, critical success factors and so on.

3.11 The **strategic objectives** of the purchasing function. If cost reduction is the priority, purchasing may be centralised to enable economies of scale, for example. If customer service is a priority, it may be decentralised to allow responsive 'local' decision-making, or organised by customer group. If supply performance is a priority, the function may be organised by commodity (for specialisation) or supplier group (for better relationship management). And so on.

3.12 *Lysons and Farrington* highlight two further key structural issues for purchasing and supply.

- Increasing focus on business processes and supply chains, leading to the increasing integration of supply activities and the creation of 'horizontal' (cross-functional and inter-organisational) structures
- The existence of diversified and/or geographically dispersed multi-SBU organisations, raising the decision of whether to centralise or decentralise.

Procurement and supply's responsibilities

3.13 The responsibilities of the purchasing function can be analysed according to strategic (long-term), tactical (medium-term), and operational (daily) responsibilities. These are set out in Table 3.2.

Table 3.2 *The responsibilities of a purchasing function*

STRATEGIC RESPONSIBILITIES	TACTICAL RESPONSIBILITIES	OPERATIONAL RESPONSIBILITIES
Developing guidelines and procedures	Preparing specifications	Preparing orders
Developing performance monitoring systems	Preparing value analysis programmes	Expediting
Major sourcing decisions, such as single vs multiple sourcing, reciprocal trading	Selecting and contracting with suppliers	Monitoring and evaluating supplier performance
Major decisions relating to capital investment or make-or-buy	Preparing certification programmes for suppliers	
Establishing long-term partnership and co-makership relations	Agreement on corporate and/or annual supplier agreements	

Figure 3.6 *The widening spectrum of purchasing activities*

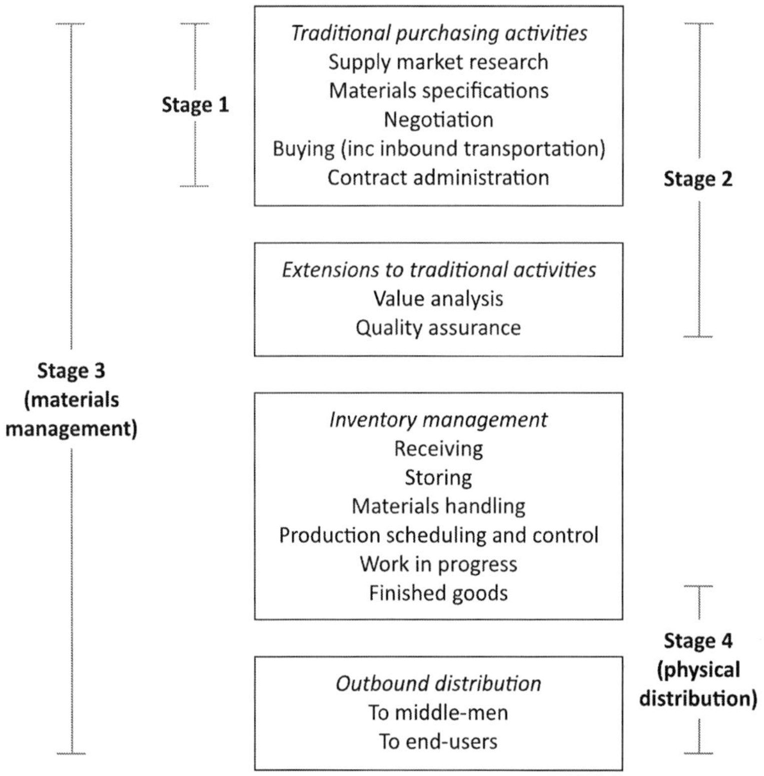

Purchasing as a subsidiary function

3.14 So far we have assumed that there is a dedicated purchasing function in the organisation. But what if there is not?

3.15 In such cases, purchasing usually reports through another functional head, and there are generally three possibilities.

- **Production/operations**. The focus of attention for any purchasing activity will be on production-related logistical difficulties. Purchasing will be unlikely to make a valuable contribution to design, marketing and competitiveness, given that it will not secure the involvement of suppliers in value engineering, value analysis or bidders' conferences.

- **Finance**. Reporting through the finance department can suppress the purchasing professional's creativity. Responsibility for purchasing expenditure and the management of supplier credit can be used as crude short-term braking mechanisms, which in turn stifle partnership arrangements and can jeopardise long-term goals and aspirations for strategic purchasing activities.
- **Commercial**. This probably represents the best choice from a bad lot. A commercial director who also acts as purchasing manager should have individual responsibility for the final decision on proposals and quotations. There should be a formal set of procedures to examine the appropriateness of any bid to overall corporate strategy.

Chapter summary

- In all but the very smallest organisations, it is necessary to 'differentiate' by dividing tasks up among different individuals and departments. At the same time, it is necessary to 'integrate' by means of co-ordinating mechanisms.
- Possible organisation structures include functional, geographical, product, matrix and hybrid structures.
- Although buyers operate in a procurement and supply function, it is important to know about the work carried out by other functions such as production, marketing etc.
- In recent decades, the strategic importance of the procurement function has increasingly been recognised.

Self-test questions

Numbers in brackets refer to the paragraphs where you can check your answers.

1 Explain what Lawrence and Lorsch mean by 'differentiation' and 'integration' in organisations. (1.2, 1.3)

2 Sketch an organisation arranged on functional lines. (Figure 3.1)

3 What is meant by 'divisionalisation'? (1.16)

4 Explain how a matrix structure works. (1.18)

5 Briefly summarise the role of (a) the production department and (b) the marketing and sales department. (2.1, 2.9)

6 What are the three hierarchical levels at which purchasing may operate, according to Lysons? (3.3)

7 List factors that influence the design of the purchasing function. (3.7ff)

CHAPTER 4

Mission Statements and Beyond

Assessment criteria and indicative content

2.1 Describe the use of mission and vision statements and objectives by a procurement and supply function

- Objectives of procurement and supply functions
- Targets for procurement and supply functions
- Use of mission and vision statements for procurement and supply functions

Section headings

1 Aligning with corporate objectives
2 Objectives for procurement and supply
3 Performance targets for procurement and supply
4 Mission and vision statements

1 Aligning with corporate objectives

Recap: the hierarchy of objectives

1.1 In Chapter 2, we discussed performance measures for the purchasing and supply function as a whole. We saw that they were based on the 'cascade' of objectives from the corporate level to the functional level. From there, the cascade continues on down to the level of the individual.

1.2 The objectives of an individual buyer should support the objectives of the purchasing and supply function, which in turn support the objectives of the organisation. Individual performance measures will therefore, to a large extent, reflect purchasing and supply performance measures in areas such as productivity, profitability, cost-reduction, internal customer satisfaction, effective supplier relations and partnering, ethical and environmental sourcing and so on.

1.3 In Chapter 2, we looked at the hierarchy of objectives from organisation mission to operational plans and action targets, and how they should be aligned both vertically and horizontally. Refer back to that material if you need to, but it is summarised in Figure 4.1.

1.4 Vertical alignment is required to ensure that all sub-unit efforts contribute to overall corporate mission, for unity of direction, while horizontal alignment is required to ensure that the efforts of different sub-units dovetail with each other, for co-ordinated effort and a coherent face to the world.

Figure 4.1 *Individual and team objectives*

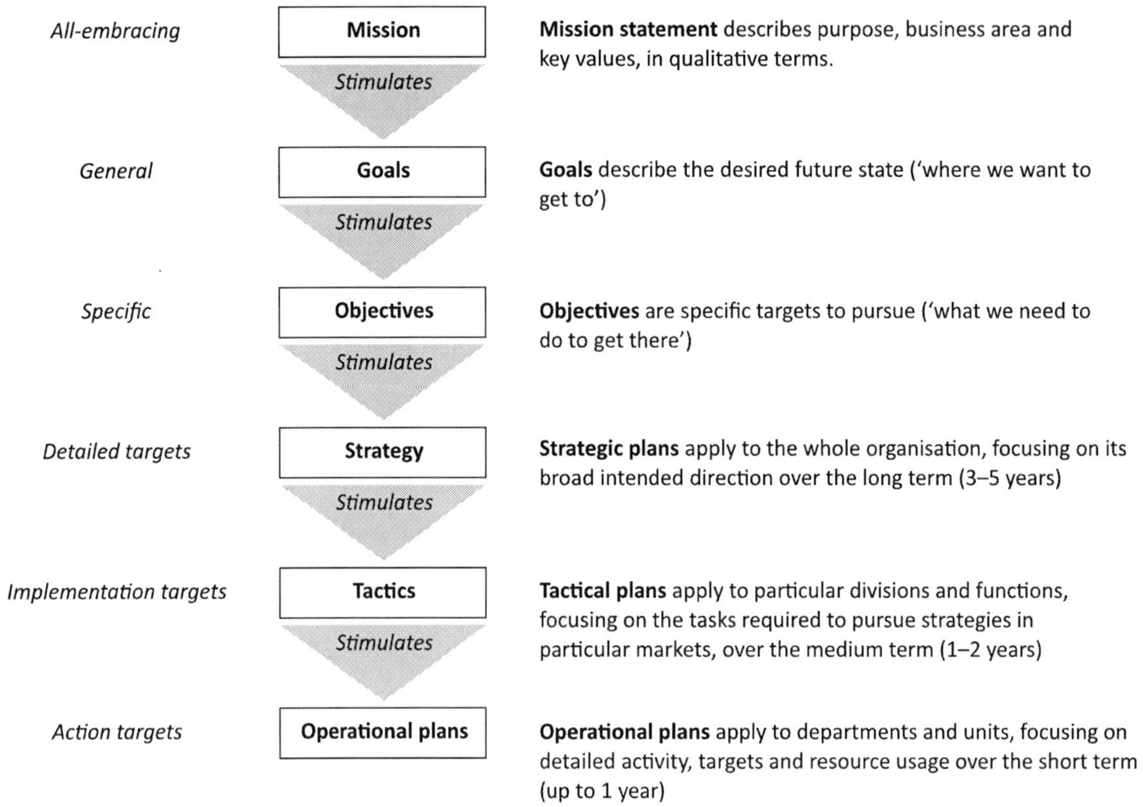

1.5 As the hierarchy of planning suggests, objectives are set at a number of levels. At the departmental or functional level (discussed in Chapter 2), they set out the specific targets or key results to be achieved by the function in order to contribute to strategic plans. At the team level, they set out the key results or contribution expected of the team, in order to achieve departmental goals. And at the individual level, they are job-related or role-related: what results are individuals expected to achieve, to what standard, in what key activity areas, in order for all the higher objectives to be achieved?

Management by objectives (MbO)

1.6 As you might imagine, integrating objectives throughout the 'cascade' of objectives is not easy to achieve. One suggested method for accomplishing this is management by objectives. MbO is a systematic approach to integrating individual, functional and corporate plans: a process whereby individual goals are integrated with the corporate plan, as part of an ongoing programme of goal-setting and performance review involving all levels of management.

1.7 The steps in an MbO process are as follows.

- Develop a coherent strategic plan, with clear organisational goals and objectives
- Collaboratively define each individual's major areas of responsibility and the purpose of their role within the corporate plan
- Jointly define and agree the key tasks which are directly related to the achievement of the objectives, and in which any performance shortfall would negatively impact on success
- Jointly define and agree, for each key task, key results (which must be achieved in order for the key tasks to be successfully performed and objectives met) and methods of monitoring and measuring performance in these areas (key performance indicators)

- Agree individual (or unit) performance improvement plans for a defined planning period: selecting specific improvement objectives for each key task and formulating action plans to achieve those objectives.
- Implement monitoring, self-evaluation and periodic review of performance at agreed intervals, and revise objectives, targets and action plans as required.

1.8 Advocates of MbO argue that such a process is helpful in clarifying organisational and unit goals; focusing attention on priority areas; systematically converting strategic plans into co-ordinated managerial action plans and budgets; securing the involvement and commitment of individuals to defined targets and areas of accountability; and supplying systematic information for managerial planning and control, individual performance appraisal and development planning.

1.9 Critics of MbO argue that there is a danger of rigidity because of the effort and investment put into integrated planning. Plans must be flexible – especially in complex and dynamic environments (where objectives may change) and in flexible work roles (where individual contributions may vary with requirements). There may be employee relations problems, if staff perceive that they are being made more accountable for performance without a corresponding increase in empowerment or involvement.

1.10 Introducing MbO may require a significant change in organisation structure, management style and culture. It needs to be supported and sustained by senior management.

Purchasing roles and corporate objectives

1.11 The individual components of a purchasing job link to the overall objectives of the organisation, in three key areas.

- **Contribution of individuals to an organisation's profitability**
  Individual buyers can contribute measurably to savings on materials, inventory, contract and transaction costs (eg through effective negotiation and contract development, efficient conduct of the purchasing cycle, and effective use of inventory management and e-procurement tools). These savings in turn contribute to bottom line profit.

  If cost reductions are retained within the business, there is an immediate improvement in the bottom line. If the surplus resource is used up by budget holders, there is no direct impact on the bottom line – but there is still added benefit.

  It should also be noted that profitability is not solely based on price: the total cost of ownership (or acquisition) of capital items, for example, includes delivery, support, consumables, staff training, inventory and handling costs, inspection, maintenance and repair and so on. Individuals therefore have an impact on profitability through their long-term decisions about quality, supply reliability, supplier selection and so on.
- **Management of basic purchasing workload**
  Individual buyers can contribute meaningfully to the provision of the 'five rights' of purchasing: ensuring that materials of the right quality are delivered in the right quantity at the right place at the right time for the right price (and arguably also from the right source).

  The efficiency and effectiveness with which individuals carry out their own role and workload contributes to the attainment of the operational objectives of the purchasing and supply function, in areas such as procurement, stores and inventory management, support for quality and production management, storage and distribution of finished goods, transport management, customer and supplier relationship management, outsourcing (external organisation) management and so on.

- **Development of purchasing infrastructure and competency**
  Individual buyers can contribute meaningfully to the development and improvement of the purchasing function: its structure, culture, competence, body of knowledge and status or visibility in the organisation.
  Individual objectives support this contribution in areas such as strategic awareness, personal effectiveness, networking and relationships with key stakeholders (suppliers, internal customers, budget holders, line unit buyers, contractors), the effective use of e-procurement technologies and the continual undertaking of learning and professional development activities.

2 Objectives for procurement and supply

Why are individual objectives important?

2.1 Setting effective goals and objectives – at all levels – is important for organisational reasons.

- They promote unity of direction, aiding co-ordination and efficient organisation: reducing overlaps and gaps in activity
- They enable limited resources to be intentionally allocated to optimise corporate performance (rather than potentially sub-optimal performance due to competition between units and individuals)
- They provide an objective measure against which performance can be evaluated and accountability maintained
- They support flexibility, by focusing on key end results or critical success factors, rather than inputs (which may change) and processes (which may cause a bureaucratic, inward focus).

2.2 Goal-setting is also important, at an individual and team level, for behavioural reasons.

- Goals enable tasks to be broken down into manageable, time-bounded 'chunks', while at the same time giving people a sense of their role and contribution to the whole activity of the organisation.
- Goals are important in motivation: people are motivated by the decision that it is worth expending effort to reach desired outcomes (goals), and by feedback information telling them to what extent they have achieved those goals. For the same reason, goals are also vital in learning and change.

Setting effective objectives

2.3 In order to be effective, individual objectives must be effectively formulated. A popular framework for evaluating objectives is SMART – although we prefer an extended or SMARTER version: Table 4.1. (This is a reminder of what you have already seen in Chapter 2.)

Table 4.1 *SMARTER objectives*

Specific	Stated in clear, detailed terms: precisely what the desired outcomes or deliverables are
Measurable	Susceptible to monitoring, review and measurement (ideally in quantitative or numerical terms) so that we know when or how far progress/success has been attained
Attainable	Target outcomes and standards, and the contexts and timetables within which they must be attained, must be realistically achievable, using the capacities, capabilities, readiness and resources available
Relevant	The objectives must be relevant to the strategic objectives of the unit and the business as a whole: they must lead somewhere meaningful
Time-bounded	Target timescales and deadlines for completion (or review) must be included in the objective: it is not open ended
Evaluated	The objective must have been assessed as worth pursuing, given the investment in time or effort it will require: this may involve some form of cost-benefit analysis
Responsible	The objective must take into account potential impacts on key stakeholders, in the light of the unit's (and organisation's) ethical responsibilities towards them

2.4 The following is an example for a buyer's role.

Key task: Improve efficiency and productivity in purchase ordering

Objective: Increase productivity of purchase order generation by 5%

Performance measures:
- Purchase orders per employee
- Cost per purchase order
- Hours required to complete a requisition and purchase order
- % of purchase orders communicated electronically to suppliers

Timescale: December 20XX: review monthly

2.5 Eight to ten well-formulated objectives may be realistic for any given planning and control period.

2.6 Common problems with objectives and objective-setting, which must be addressed by managers, include: constantly changing focus and targets (or, conversely, failure to review and adjust targets); poorly-constructed (un-SMART) objectives; a limited range of objectives (neglecting qualitative criteria such as ethics and relationships); not enough flexibility within the boundaries set by objectives; inadequate information for, or attention to, measuring performance against objectives; and setting too few or insufficiently challenging objectives.

3 Performance targets for procurement and supply

A range of individual performance measures

3.1 Managers may use a range of performance measures (at any level).

- External measures such as: internal customer satisfaction, external customer satisfaction, number and type of quality or delivery complaints
- Operational measures such as: on-time in-full deliveries, number and type of errors or defects, facility and equipment utilisation, productivity
- Financial measures such as costs of labour, processing, procurement and inventory, cost reductions, operating profit and profit per customer
- Development measures such as number of suggestions and improvements, training hours, involvement in quality teams.

Statistical performance measures (or metrics)

3.2 In its guide *Performance Measurement of the Procurement Profession*, CIPS Australia argues that: 'Historically, procurement performance has been focused on 'cost' or 'savings'. This narrow approach fails to address the trade-offs with quality, inventory and supplier relationships (to name a few). Due to increased focus on business results, performance measurement has been extended to broader business (risk, inventory) and operational objectives (percentage of spend)... The incentive for applying a robust performance measurement system is that both the procurement function and the broader organisation will benefit from enhanced appreciation of procurement contributions.'

3.3 Table 4.2 shows some of the quantified performance metrics which might form part of such a robust system. Although some of these refer to the purchasing function as a whole, you should be able to pick out those which could also be used as individual measures, or to which individual contribution might be assessed.

Table 4.2 *Performance metrics for purchasing*

EFFICIENCY METRICS	
Cost	Procurement cost as a % of spend
Staffing	Staff per $million of spend Labour cost per employee % of training, development and improvement targets met
Productivity	Purchase orders or material receipts per employee Cost per purchase order or receipt
Technology leverage and integration	Technology cost as a % of procurement cost % of automatic (v manual) transactions % of purchase orders communicated electronically to suppliers or potential suppliers
Cycle time	Hours required to complete a requisition and purchase order Overall lead time (from requisition to receipt)
Standardisation	Use of company-wide policies, commodity codes
EFFECTIVENESS METRICS	
Cost savings	Annual cost savings or margin contribution as a % of spend Price paid against standard or market indices Prices paid against budget
Inventory	% inventory reduction Number of product stockouts and emergency orders Comparison of stock with target stock
Supplier leverage	Number of suppliers per $x of spend % of suppliers providing 80% or more of the annual spend % of purchases made from preferred suppliers
Error rates	% of transactions requiring correction after process
Customer satisfaction	% of deliveries received on time in full (OTIF) Number of complaints and queries received
Strategic alignment	% of objectives linked to business strategy % of procurement time spent on global/enterprise-wide focus
Compliance	% of environmental and ethical targets met
Projects	% of milestones met % of deliverables achieved to stakeholder satisfaction

3.4 In addition, there will be a range of qualitative measures, such as: effective contribution to cross-functional teamworking in supplier development, sourcing and negotiation; satisfaction of internal and external customers (or project stakeholders); personal and skill development; contribution to particular initiatives or goals (eg quality or service improvements, make or buy decisions, outsourcing management or innovation); effectiveness of supplier and customer relationship management; impact on corporate strategic objectives and so on.

3.5 Arjen Van Weele also points out that different performance measures will be used, depending on the role of the purchasing function in the organisation. If its role is perceived as primarily administrative, measures such as lead times, productivity and error rates may be used. If its role is primarily commercial, cost savings will be a priority. At a more strategic level, from a supply chain perspective, emphasis will shift to higher measures such as strategic alignment, partnering, supplier leverage and so on.

4 Mission and vision statements

Corporate mission statements

4.1 A corporate mission statement is a statement in writing that describes the basic purpose of an organisation, that is, what it is trying to accomplish. If the mission of the organisation is subject to change there can be considerable disturbances within the organisation.

4.2 A mission statement is normally very general and visionary (hence the alternative term **vision statement**). It should be viewed as stating where the organisation is conceived to be throughout time rather than where it currently is or where it wants to get to at any one moment in time.

4.3 A mission statement may be primarily directed towards the employees of an organisation and should assist in the attainment of the organisation's objectives. It will have some or all of the following characteristics.

- It is usually a brief statement of not more than a page in length; some companies have produced very effective mission statements comprising a single sentence.
- It is a very general statement of entity culture.
- It states the aims or purposes of the organisation.
- It states the business areas in which the organisation intends to operate.
- It is open-ended (not stated in quantifiable terms).
- It does not include commercial terms, such as profit.
- It is not time-assigned. Some organisations still have mission statements written decades ago.
- It forms a basis of communication to the people inside the organisation and to people outside.
- It is used as a starting point for formulating goals, objectives and short-term targets.

4.4 In constructing a mission statement, it is worthwhile noting that the following features are usually present.

- The organisation's reason for existence (the corporate purpose)
- The business domain in which the organisation will operate (the corporate scope)
- The stakeholder groups the organisation will serve

4.5 A corporate mission statement is closely linked with the organisation's goals and objectives. Before setting about the preparation of a strategic plan the management should consider the mission statement. Many commentators have suggested that drawing up the mission statement is the essential first step in the strategic planning process.

4.6 Mission statements can provide motivation to the employees of the organisation in the sense that they tell people what is important to the top layers of management. Decision making processes within an organisation should be improved as a result of clarifying of the organisation's overall direction.

Mission and vision statements for procurement and supply

4.7 Mission and vision statements focus on the business at a strategic level, and may have little obvious relevance to staff in a particular department. Many larger organisations and some government bodies have found that departmental mission and vision statements are effective in communicating and setting the direction for the department.

4.8 Many departments, not only procurement and supply, have issued mission and vision statements. These statements incorporate the purpose and scope of the organisational mission and vision statements but focus on the particular department, its role and purpose in the company and how it intends to fulfil that role.

4.9 As suppy chain management has become a more strategic activity in companies in recent years it is only natural that the departmental mission statement and vision statement should be developed and issued.

4.10 The organisational mission and vision statements can appear distant to many of those down the chain of command in an organisation. A procurement and supply mission and vision statement allows managers to adapt the key aspects of the organisational mission statement in a way that has a direct relevance to the procurement and supply department.

4.11 In this way the mission statement can be read and understood by those in the department while the vision statement looks towards the future. Particularly in the case of supply chain management the vision statement can prove particularly relevant in such a fast changing business area.

4.12 The internet holds many purchasing and procurement mission statements. It is worth spending a few minutes browsing and comparing them. As an example, the Department of Purchasing and Supply Management of Fairfax County, Virginia USA, publishes the following mission and vision statement.

- MISSION – The Department is committed to providing the necessary resources that establish a foundation for quality service to the community
- VISION – The Department strives to join with vendors and County departments to secure quality goods and services in a timely manner and at a reasonable cost while ensuring that all purchasing actions are conducted fairly and impartially.

4.13 These statements are then supported by a list of 'values' related to customer care, accurate and timely information, effective partnerships, innovation, and open access to procurement opportunities.

Chapter summary

- Integrating objectives through all levels of an organisation is a complex task. Management by objectives (MbO) is one model for achieving this.
- Setting goals and objectives at all levels is important for both organisational reasons and behavioural reasons.
- Effective objectives are SMART (or SMARTER). Evaluated + Responsible.
- It is important to set performance measures for purchasing and supply. These should cover both efficiency and effectiveness.
- A corporate mission statement may not have obvious relevance to any particular department within the organisation. For this reason, many departments develop their own mission and vision statements.

Self-test questions

Numbers in brackets refer to the paragraphs where you can check your answers.

1 What is meant by 'management by objectives'? (1.6)

2 List steps in an MbO process. (1.7)

3 Suggest (a) organisational reasons and (b) behavioural reasons why goal-setting is important. (2.1, 2.2)

4 List possible performance metrics for purchasing efficiency and effectiveness. (Table 4.2)

5 List typical characteristics of a corporate mission statement. (4.3)

6 Why is it sometimes thought necessary to develop departmental mission statements? (4.7)

CHAPTER 5

Key Roles of Procurement and Supply

Assessment criteria and indicative content

2.2 Describe the main roles and structures of a procurement and supply function within an organisation

- Links to organisational goals
- Competition and regulatory roles
- Advice and guidance that a procurement and supply function can provide to other functions
- Procurement and supply as a service function
- Centralised, devolved and lead buying structures of procurement and supply functions

Section headings

1 Links to organisational goals
2 Competition and regulatory roles
3 Advice and guidance for other functions
4 Procurement and supply as a service function
5 Structures of procurement and supply functions

1 Links to organisational goals

1.1 Plans vary in the level at which they are taken, the breadth of the business they cover, the detail they examine and the length of their horizon (or how far ahead they look).

- Corporate strategies apply to the whole organisation. They focus on the broad, general direction of the organisation, and how value will be added, over the long term (say, 3–5 years)
- Tactical or business level strategies apply to particular divisions, functions or strategic business units. They focus on the tasks and objectives required to pursue the chosen corporate strategies and compete successfully in particular markets, over the medium term (say, 1–2 years).
- Operational or functional strategies and plans apply to functions and departments. They focus on the specific detail of tasks, targets, resources and actions needed to deliver the corporate and business level strategies, over the short term (up to a year, say).

1.2 In practice, this neat division between three levels of strategy is complicated by overlapping strategic concerns. Moreover, strategy does not always flow down the levels; strategies may also emerge from the bottom up. For example, a purchasing function might pioneer new approaches to supplier relations (because of built-up trust, or advantageous supply market conditions, say) – and these relationships might stimulate and open up the possibility of total quality management at the corporate level.

1.3 Thirdly, objectives should – where possible – be formulated with the participation or at least the agreement of key stakeholders, including team members who will have to implement changes, in order to secure buy-in and commitment.

Integrating supply chain strategies

1.4 Planning a strategy for managing the supply chain is essentially a process similar to planning an overall corporate strategy: environmental, organisational and functional analysis; the definition of objectives; the identification, evaluation and selection of strategic options; and the implementation of the chosen strategy.

1.5 It is in identifying objectives and identifying strategic options that the link is clearest between functional and corporate strategy. Supply chain objectives and proposed strategies must be compatible with the corporate strategy: various formal and informal processes (discussed a bit later) may be used to bring the two into step.

1.6 Specific areas where corporate objectives and purchasing objectives can be clearly seen to be interlinked are shown in Table 5.1.

Table 5.1 *Links between corporate and purchasing objectives*

CORPORATE OBJECTIVES	PURCHASING OBJECTIVES
Maintain or increase market share	Provide supplies to match customer needs; assure quality; reduce delivery lead time; reduce cost
Improve profits, cashflow, and return on capital	Reduce stocks; improve reliability; more frequent deliveries
Shorten time to market	Early supplier involvement; simultaneous engineering
Eliminate non-core activities	Develop effective make-or-buy policy; integrate purchasing and capacity planning
Introduce continuous improvement	Reduce supplier base; partnership and co-makership approaches; reduce product complexity; increase accuracy and reliability
Become world class supplier	Work with suppliers to establish world class standards; improve flexibility of response to market conditions; liaison with technological sources

Integrating processes

1.7 Various formal and informal processes may be implemented to ensure that supply chain strategies are integrated with corporate strategy.

- A formal long-term procurement plan may be developed as part of the corporate planning process (or as a component of a business strategy)
- Purchasing managers may be involved in the corporate planning process: through representation on the main board of directors, or less formally by consultation, networking and political influence
- The main board of directors may act as an integrating mechanism, providing guidance on corporate strategy and direction (in the form of organisation-wide policies on ethics, the environment, intra-company trading, international sourcing and so on), and retaining power of authorisation over supply chain strategy

- Interpersonal relations between purchasing managers and a supportive chief executive may informally facilitate integration, as information is exchanged about objectives and environmental threats and opportunities.

1.8 Other integrating factors in the organisational context include the following.

- Recent decades have seen the integration of materials-handling functions across an increasingly wide span of the value chain: from purchasing to materials management, to logistics management and finally to supply chain management. This supports strategic alignment in two ways. As a process-oriented view, it focuses attention on the interdependence of functional strategies and decisions. And integrated IT systems for supply and logistics can be further integrated into the overall corporate management information system.
- The cost savings available from consolidating or aggregating the purchasing requirements of SBUs through a centralised procurement function places purchasing strategy a step closer to overall corporate strategy.
- Strategic purchasing requirements (taking into account the importance to the organisation of the item being purchased and the risk and complexity of the supply market) are the basis of procurement strategies.
- Purchasing and supply management has increasingly embraced areas of strategic concern at the corporate level: make/do or buy decisions, quality management, corporate social responsibility (including ethical sourcing and sustainable trading) and environmental issues (reduced packaging, recyclable materials, reverse logistics capability and so on).

Strategic implications of supply chain management (SCM)

1.9 A strategic SCM approach thus implies the need to develop strategies for:

- The role and positioning of an organisation within the total supply chain (eg through forward or backward integration)
- The configuration of the chain or network, and the competitive or collaborative nature of the relationships within it
- The selection of strategic supply chain partners. (A co-operative SCM network will not include all suppliers: resources will be focused on the relations that are of strategic importance for the competitiveness of the business.)
- Internal and trans-organisational processes for materials and information flow: process structure, production and distribution flows, planning and control systems, information systems and so on.
- Collaborative and integrative arrangements (eg joint planning and control systems, cross-training of staff, relationship-specific technologies), where appropriate.

1.10 *Lambert, Cooper and Pagh* express these considerations as three interconnected components: Figure 5.1.

Figure 5.1 *Components of SCM*

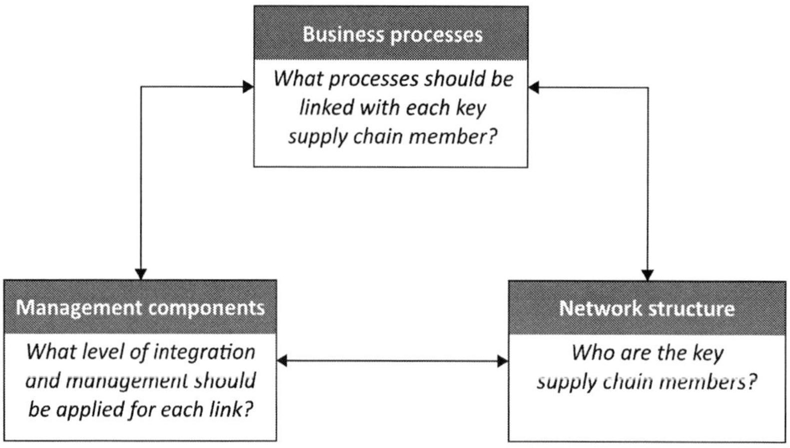

2 Competition and regulatory roles

The competition role of procurement and supply

2.1 Competition can be a crucial factor in driving economic growth in an economy. It will impact on both efficiency and innovation. The role of competition in driving economic growth is particularly important when growth is slow and financial constraints are being applied.

2.2 Within organisations, competition acts as a disciplining device, placing pressure on managers to become more efficient. Competition ensures that those companies with higher productivity will increase their market share at the expense of those who are less productive. Competition also encourages companies to innovate in the creation of new products and services.

2.3 Competition can also contribute to growth in other ways, most notably by bringing down costs both within companies and across companies. Working more closely with suppliers can lead to the benefits that come from competition being channelled toward a mutually beneficial working relationship.

Supplier development

2.4 Supplier development is an activity that a buyer undertakes to improve a supplier's performance and/or capabilities to meet the buyer's short-term supply needs. These activities include the assessment of a supplier's operation, providing incentives to improve performance, fostering competition among suppliers and working directly with suppliers, through training or other activities.

2.5 Supplier development involves financial and personnel commitment from both companies, the sharing of information and the creation of an effective means of measuring performance.

2.6 Supplier development plays an important role as supply chains become more integrated. For many manufacturing companies over 50% of their revenue is spent on purchases. Consequently suppliers will have a greater impact on the quality, cost, technology and delivery of the buying company's own products and services, and hence in its profitability.

2.7 Many manufacturing firms are outsourcing (subcontracting) parts and services to focus on their core competencies. They expect their suppliers to deliver innovative and quality products on time at a competitive cost. When a supplier is not capable of meeting these needs, the buyer can bring the outsourced item in house and produce it internally or switch over to a more capable supplier or help improve the existing supplier's capabilities. All of these can work. The choice depends on price, volume or the strategic nature of the procured item.

2.8 Continuous long-term improvement of supplier performance is only achieved by:

- Identifying where value is created in the supply chain
- Positioning the buyer strategically in line with value creation
- Implementing an integrated supply chain management strategy to maximise internal and external capabilities throughout the supply chain

2.9 The nature of competition for the purchaser has changed in recent years. It is no longer a case of comparing quotes and adopting an adversarial stance toward suppliers. To leverage the maximum gains it will often involve working more closely with suppliers and developing a mutual understanding of each other's company and culture in order to gain the maximum benefits.

2.10 We will have more to say about the competition role of procurement in the next chapter.

The regulatory role of procurement and supply

2.11 The regulatory role of procurement and supply refers to rules laid down by the department in relation to operational practice. A detailed **purchasing policy manual** will address the regulations and roles relating to the procurement process of an organisation. The manual will add detail in regard to operational processes. The manual is categorised under a number of headings, which we will summarise below. The manual serves to detail the role of purchasing within an organisation and the operating practices consistent with company or government policies.

2.12 We will look at the style of a public sector policy manual. The basic layout is equally applicable to the private sector.

2.13 **Introduction and scope.** The manual provides guidance on the rules that apply to staff involved in the procurement activity. Adherence to the policies set out in the manual is mandatory.

2.14 **Definition.** Procurement is the process of buying goods, services and works from external suppliers. The procurement process begins when a need to buy something is identified and will generally end after the contract has been awarded. Contract management will be carried out throughout the duration of the contract.

2.15 **Procurement roles, responsibilities and compliance.** The purchasing profession has a whole range of different job titles depending on the elements required for each post. Most companies will have a 'model' that works best for them, but here are some of the job titles that you may come across.

- Procurement officer
- Buyer
- Supply chain manager
- Supplier relationship manager
- Contract manager
- Category buyer

- Purchasing manager
- E-procurement manager
- Assistant buyer

2.16 These job titles will have defined roles and responsibilities within a reporting hierarchy. However, the business goals and strategies will be dictated by the sector they are in, whether public, private, or not-for-profit. The manual may require details of the roles and responsibilities of these positions together with the title given to each job in the company or organisation. A job description will refine the duties and responsibilities further.

2.17 **Delegated purchasing authority**. Delegated purchasing authority (DPA) is the authority to enter into a contract for goods, services and works and to oversee the process leading up to and including the award of a contract and any subsequent contract changes.

2.18 DPA is granted to permanent staff only and will be in writing based on the business need and the training and experience of staff concerned. It will specify the value of contracts that the individual will be authorised to award. DPA is intended to allow business units the opportunity to manage requirements within the business area.

2.19 DPA is personal to an individual only whilst occupying their current position. DPA does not automatically transfer to their successor should they leave their current position, nor does it transfer with them to another position. If DPA is to be withdrawn by the Director for any reason this will be confirmed in writing.

2.20 **Commitment to a contract**. A contract is a legally binding agreement between the organisation and one or more suppliers for the supply of specified goods, services and works. The contract sets out the details of what the organisation is buying from whom and the rights and obligations of the parties.

2.21 **Separation of duties**. Organisation policy may well require that there are at least two defined roles in the procurement process.

- The budget holder or customer who perceives the need and makes out the business case to obtain any necessary approval to spend
- The Delegated Purchasing Officer (DPO) who is responsible for ensuring that the procurement process fully complies with procurement policy

2.22 **Ethical standards**. Organisation policy may well require that staff must preserve the highest standards of honesty, integrity, impartiality and objectivity in all dealings with suppliers and potential suppliers.

3 Advice and guidance for other functions

3.1 Internal consultants are often called in to solve a particular problem or fulfil a need that cannot be efficiently or effectively satisfied with the internal resources and expertise of the client unit. The purchasing function may adopt an internal consultancy role in an organisation when:

- Procurement activity is undertaken by 'part-time' buyers or non-purchasing staff in user departments or budget-holder departments. Since these staff may lack the specialist skills, disciplines and contacts for effective and cost-efficient purchasing, the advice and guidance of purchasing professionals may be required.

- Procurement is required for a multi-functional project. The purchasing function is ideally placed to research and recommend procurement solutions.
- Specific disciplines, skills or information are required by other functions, project teams or managers, which purchasing is in a position to contribute. Purchasing may be asked to provide advice or training for sales personnel in negotiation techniques, say; or may be asked to act as introducers and facilitators, putting the product development team in touch with potential supply partners; or may be asked to carry out a benchmarking exercise on competitors' logistics or quality management processes.
- Purchasing lacks the formal organisational authority (mandate) to impose purchasing disciplines, procedures or decisions on other departments – and must therefore exercise influence by promoting its value-adding expertise.

3.2 Internal consultancy – in the sense of offering other departments the benefit of procurement's specialist expertise – may also operate through a variety of operational mechanisms.

- Established procurement policies and procedures – acting as guidelines for buyers in other departments, to help them source and purchase inputs more cost-effectively and with less risk
- Preferred and approved supplier lists, framework agreements and call-off contracts – ensuring that buyers in other departments use suppliers pre-selected (and agreements negotiated) using purchasing expertise
- Purchasing research and information (eg supply market or category updates) – providing planners and buyers with relevant data to support their decisions, based on purchasing's in-depth knowledge and contacts
- Standard terms and conditions in supply contracts – managing risk by providing sound contract terms and minimising the risk of legal problems
- Negotiation services and skills – conducting negotiations on behalf of other departments, or advising and training them in negotiation skills, as a way of maximising the organisation's share of value from transactions and relationships
- Supplier and supplier relationship management – creating and developing sources of collaboration and information which may benefit other organisational activities.

5

3.3 Specific tasks that procurement and supply can undertake for other functions, or can assist other functions with, are listed below.

- **Purchasing.** At an operational level, the purchasing manager may, especially in a small department, fulfil the purchaser's role. Even in a larger function, the manager may perform purchasing tasks, perhaps for large capital items, contracts over a certain value, or key suppliers. The purchaser's task can be summed up as ensuring, by ethical means, the best value and quality at the lowest price.
- **Managing resources.** At a tactical level, managers must ensure that resources are acquired and deployed with maximum efficiency, for the effective achievement of corporate objectives. This includes planning and controlling the use of key resources such as: time (the manager's time, machine time and labour hours); finance (with attention to cost, efficiency, risk and the need for budgetary planning and control); physical resources (storage space, machinery and equipment, the transport fleet, raw materials and parts); and people (the skills, knowledge, experience and labour hours of purchasing and supply staff).
- **Advising on purchasing and supply systems.** At a tactical level, management also involves developing systems and procedures to enable strategic objectives to be fulfilled. Purchasing and supply managers need to develop effective information, purchasing, quality, materials management, transport and other systems, in order to ensure a flow of materials and services

to meet the organisation's needs. Because these systems affect (or will be implemented and used by) other departments and links in the supply chain, managers may not have the *authority* to impose systems, procedures, standards or controls, but may have the *influence* (by virtue of their specialist expertise) to recommend them, and advise on their design and implementation.

- **Building supply chain relationships.** This is an increasingly important role at all levels of the purchasing and supply function. At a strategic level, the building of co-operative, mutually beneficial (and therefore potentially long-lasting) relationships with the supply chain supports competitive advantage (on the basis of supply, quality or price), new product development and 'make or buy' decisions. At a tactical level, building effective relationships with existing sources, and developing alternative or additional sources (to meet unforeseen contingencies and planned needs) is essential to secure continuity of supply. Meanwhile, at an operational level, effective communication and trust supports the day-to-day planning, co-ordination and control of supply chain activity.
- **Policy development.** 'Policies' are broad statements of intent which translate strategies into guidelines for management decision-making. They allow managers to exercise their own discretion, but within clearly understood parameters. Managers in purchasing and supply will have expert input to the formulation of policies in regard to matters such as: environmental responsibility; ethical trading; quality management; and 'make or buy' decisions.
- **Quality.** 'It is the buyer's responsibility to ensure that suppliers possess the ability, the motivation and adequate information to produce materials and components of the specified quality in a cost-effective manner' (*Dobler et al).* At a strategic level, this may involve supplier relationship management, early supplier involvement, supplier selection and development policies, quality management and continuous improvement strategies and the establishment of systems for controlling supplier performance.
- **Cost reduction and control.** This may involve: contribution to make/do or buy and investment decisions; the application of value analysis and engineering; the development of sourcing strategies to reduce materials costs (eg by price leverage or variety reduction), transaction and contracting costs (eg fewer small orders, preferred suppliers) and stock holding costs (eg minimal inventory, just in time); contribution to quality strategies (reducing inspection and defect costs); management of supplier relationships and contracts (to ensure cost advantages and invite collaboration in cost reduction); and computerisation of processes (materials handling, e-sourcing and e-procurement, transport planning and so on).
- **Innovation**. This requires the development of supply chains that are primarily market-responsive, rather than physically efficient; sourcing strategies which reduce lead times; supplier selection on the basis of speed, flexibility and quality; inventory strategies enabling response to unpredictable demand (eg buffer stocks of parts or finished goods).
- **Delivery**. This requires: management of the supply base to minimise supplier risks (especially for critical or bottleneck items); inventory strategies to meet required service levels while minimising stock holding costs (eg JIT or buffer stock, depending on the nature of demand); distribution and transport strategies securing timely, efficient and risk-managed supply; and so on.

3.4 Purchasing may need to prove the value of its service (or present a 'business case' for its service) by collecting and presenting data on performance measures such as: fulfilment of specific agreed consultancy and performance objectives and service levels; cost reductions and/or quality improvements achieved; client compliance (eg with purchasing procedures) and satisfaction; and so on.

4 Procurement and supply as a service function

4.1 An often overlooked aspect of service delivery in business-to-business settings is the issue of service quality among internal business units. In practice many organisational departments are service providers primarily to customers within the organisation. For example, management information systems, human resources, and purchasing departments all share an important function supporting other employees as they perform their jobs.

4.2 Managers of those internal service functions are becoming more concerned with delivering high levels of service quality to their internal customers.

The internal services provided by procurement and supply

4.3 Internal service quality can be defined for this purpose as employee satisfaction with the service received from internal service providers. It is an issue that not only concerns purchasing but can be applied to other functional units such as distribution and human resources.

4.4 The role of purchasing within an organisation puts it in regular contact with both internal and external customers. Purchasing in particular is aware of customer service considerations in terms of delivery, quality, service level agreements, and key performance indicators. It is not too much of a leap to expect the quality of the purchasing department to be evaluated.

4.5 There are various measures that could be used to evaluate the effectiveness of purchasing's service to its internal customers. These include:

- Average lapse of time between requisition and delivery
- Average cost of processing a requisition through to delivery
- Number of complaints from user departments
- Cost savings achieved for user departments

Managing the internal service

4.6 If purchasing is regarded as providing a service to internal customers, then it is appropriate to manage the service, just as if we were servicing an external client. One important step to this end would be a system of measurement and control.

4.7 The task of managing the purchasing function naturally falls to the Head of Purchasing, whose task includes ensuring a quality service for internal users of the purchasing service. As part of this process, Head of Purchasing has a duty to communicate effectively with users of the purchasing service.

4.8 The process of measuring and assessing internal satisfaction with a department is quite new. If delivered to users via an IT based questionnaire the results can be quickly evaluated and should prove useful in determining the strengths and weaknesses of the department and highlighting areas of concern that may not be obvious within the department. Action can then be taken to address the identified weaknesses.

5 Structures of procurement and supply functions

Centralisation and decentralisation

5.1 An important organisational issue is the extent to which purchasing responsibilities should be centralised, ie placed in the hands of a single department reporting to a single executive.

5.2 One particular context in which this arises concerns service firms. In such firms it is common to find that purchasing is carried out by users rather than by purchasing specialists. (And this practice is by no means confined to service firms.)

5.3 This situation gives rise to no real differences of opinion in the purchasing literature: almost without exception, commentators suggest that responsibilities for purchasing should lie as far as possible with purchasing specialists. Although user departments have an important role in decision making, actual selection of suppliers and processing of orders falls to the purchasing function.

5.4 The position is far more complex when multi-site operations are in question. Clearly, an organisation that operates through a number of branches or divisions, perhaps separated by considerable distances, may consider a single purchasing function at head office (centralisation) or separate functions at each division (decentralisation). The choice is rarely clear cut, and an aim of this section of the text is to review the advantages and disadvantages of each option.

Advantages of centralisation

5.5 In most cases, both centralisation and decentralisation are realistic options. The problem then is to decide which policy offers the greater advantages. We begin by looking at the advantages of centralising the purchasing function. Later, we will consider the advantages of decentralisation.

5.6 To begin with it is worth pointing out that the choice is not necessarily between two extreme possibilities. There is a spectrum of organisational arrangements bounded at one end by full centralisation and at the other by full decentralisation. In between, there are arrangements in which some activities are centralised while other matters are decided at local level. Most organisations operate somewhere in the middle of the spectrum rather than at its extremes.

5.7 A major advantage claimed for centralisation of purchasing is the greater specialisation that is possible among purchasing staff. If 100 purchasing staff are scattered around 10 divisions each of them must have general responsibility for a wide range of his division's requirements. General responsibilities lead to general knowledge, and highly specialised knowledge may be absent.

5.8 By contrast if 100 purchasing staff are based at a single centralised location, there is opportunity to divide tasks among them on the basis of specialised skills. Each buyer can focus on a particular area and develop his knowledge to greater depth. This has great benefits when a wide range of complex materials are required by the organisation.

5.9 A further advantage is that the requirements of different divisions can be consolidated. This reduces the frequency of very small orders for a particular material and enables buyers to obtain better prices and service. The number of suppliers is likely to be smaller, and order administration and processing is more streamlined. This advantage is particularly evident if the divisions are relatively small, because in such a case there is a high likelihood that their individual requirements might be for uneconomic amounts.

5.10 Greater co-ordination of purchasing activities may result from a centralised structure. For example, uniform purchasing policies and procedures can be introduced and standardisation is facilitated. Staff training and development can be undertaken systematically.

5.11 Centralisation generally enables greater **standardisation** of procedures and specifications, avoiding 'maverick' buying.

- Standardisation of procedures should enable greater consistency of action, better performance monitoring and management (against consistent measures), better control and improved compliance.
- Standardisation of specifications should improve quality and efficiency.

5.12 Centralisation of purchasing can also avoid price anomalies between group companies or divisions. Even more importantly, it can avoid actual conflict between them in times when supplies of a particular material are scarce.

5.13 If purchasing is centralised, it is usual to establish the function at head office and to appoint an overall manager or director reporting at board level. Apart from operational buying, the function will handle planning, purchasing research, specialised buying, and negotiation of long-term contracts.

5.14 Centralised purchasing suffers from the disadvantage that communication is difficult. However, this can to some extent be countered by developing detailed purchasing manuals, arranging regular visits to divisions by central purchasing personnel, and by training courses emphasising group policies. Electronic links are also extremely important in overcoming this difficulty.

Advantages of decentralisation

5.15 Although the above considerations are powerful arguments for centralisation, things are rarely so clear cut as they might suggest. There are also significant advantages in devolving purchasing responsibilities to local level.

5.16 One reason for doing so is to maximise co-ordination between purchasing and operating departments. Buyers are close to users and develop a close understanding of their needs and problems. Face-to-face discussions are easy to organise and can help to crystallise problems and stimulate solutions.

5.17 Another benefit of decentralisation is that local buyers can respond more quickly to user needs. Centralised purchasing can run into difficulties if things do not go exactly according to plan. Reacting quickly to changes in schedules or unforeseen problems is easier if buyers are close to the scene of operations. Relying on long-distance communication inevitably means that response times are longer.

5.18 Locally based buyers also have the advantage of knowing locally based suppliers. There are great advantages – of cost, delivery time etc – in sourcing from short distances, and a centralised purchasing function will have difficulty in identifying good local suppliers.

5.19 Finally, there is an important management principle that supports a policy of decentralisation. This is the principle that a divisional manager can only be held accountable for the performance of his division if he has genuine control over its operations. This is not the case if the vitally important area of procurement is taken out of his hands and given instead to a centralised purchasing function.

5.20 If purchasing is carried out at local level, it is likely that there will still be a need for a centralised purchasing function to carry out specialised activities, such as purchasing research or buying of specialised materials. Often long-term contracts may be negotiated by the central purchasing office with divisional buyers calling off requirements against the contracts.

The lead buyer concept

5.21 A modern trend in the organisation of a purchasing function is the **centre-led action network** (CLAN). This is a relatively decentralised model that has become popular in many large organisations. Its basic principles are well explained in an article by Peter Smith in *Supply Management* (April 2003 issue). The notes below are based on Smith's article and the replies to it which appeared in subsequent issues of *Supply Management*.

5.22 According to Smith, the CLAN model is based on procurement staff located in many different business units (as opposed to a centralised model, where all or most procurement staff are located in a single unit). These staff report primarily to the local management of their business unit, though they also have a responsibility to a small procurement centre usually located at corporate HQ. This is an example of a **matrix management structure**, where some staff report to more than one boss.

5.23 The procurement centre leads the network, sets standards, encourages the spread of best practice and persuades the different elements of the network to co-operate. Often this is achieved by the concept of a **lead buyer**.

5.24 The lead buyer approach involves delegating defined purchasing responsibilities onto a designated individual within a user department. For example, a member of the manufacturing department is given responsibility for certain purchasing activities. This has the advantage that the user department is closely involved in purchasing decisions. The disadvantage is that the lead buyer is not a professional buyer.

5.25 To make this concept work, it is essential that the purchasing function give appropriate support to the lead buyer. If this is successful, the benefit is better communication and improved relations between purchasing and user departments.

Chapter summary

- When setting objectives for procurement it is important to ensure that they are aligned with the overall objectives of the organisation.
- Procurement has a role in fostering competition between suppliers so as to obtain the best possible trading terms.
- Procurement has a regulatory role in laying down procedures and standards that should be followed by all departments.
- Procurement has an internal consultancy role in providing advice and guidance to other departments.
- Procurement has a role as a supplier of services to other departments.
- An important issue to address is the extent of centralisation there should be in the management of procurement activities. Most organisations centralise some activities, while devolving others to local units.

Self-test questions

Numbers in brackets refer to the paragraphs where you can check your answers.

1 Distinguish between corporate strategies, tactical strategies and operational strategies. (1.1)

2 Give examples of links between corporate objectives and purchasing objectives. (Table 5.1)

3 Describe processes for integrating procurement strategies with corporate strategy. (1.7)

4 What is meant by supplier development? (2.4)

5 What is delegated purchasing authority? (2.17)

6 Suggest mechanisms through which purchasing may offer an internal consultancy role. (3.2)

7 List specific tasks that procurement can undertake for other functions. (3.3)

8 Suggest advantages of centralising the purchasing function. (5.5ff)

9 Suggest advantages of decentralising the purchasing function. (5.15ff)

CHAPTER 6

Key Procedures in Procurement and Supply

Assessment criteria and indicative content

2.2 Describe the main roles and structures of a procurement and supply function within an organisation

- Competition and regulatory roles

2.3 Define the main procedures that can be created by a procurement and supply function

- Delegations of authority and approvals
- Procedures that apply to running competitions between suppliers
- Auditing compliance with internal procedures

Section headings

1 Delegations of authority and approvals
2 Running competitions between suppliers
3 Auditing compliance with internal procedures

1 Delegations of authority and approvals

The impact of policy and procedure on procurement

1.1 The promotion of consistent 'good practice' (or best practice) in procurement typically involves the development and application of a range of decision rules, processes and procedures that are designed to help procurement staff to achieve their objectives.

1.2 Organisations may need to develop effective policies in regard to procurement and supply chain issues such as the following.

- An intention to comply with all relevant laws, regulations, standards, codes of practice and best practice benchmarks
- Responsibilities for procurement at different stages of the procurement process; or in cross-functional procurement teams (eg whether the organisation favours early buyer and supplier involvement in product development and specification)
- Levels of delegated authority for procurement: in other words, what levels or grades of staff have the authority to take different types of procurement decisions; when decisions need to be 'escalated' or referred; and what checks, authorisations and sign-offs are required for various tasks (such as the passing of invoices for payment)
- The use of defined procurement procedures, decision rules or guidelines to support consistent good practice (eg in areas such as the administration of tenders or e-auctions;

supplier appraisal and vendor rating; the use of approved supplier lists; or the use of call-off contracts, e-ordering systems and purchasing cards)

- Sourcing decisions (eg in regard to sustainable sourcing, single or multiple sourcing; supplier segmentation and relationship development; international or global sourcing; or the use of competitive tendering or e-auctions)
- Ethical and sustainable procurement (with objectives and commitments for local sourcing and supplier diversity; fair trade; supply chain labour standards; or 'green' specification and sourcing).

1.3 Procurement managers may have responsibility for developing some of these policies and procedures to enable strategic procurement objectives to be met. Many procurement-related policies will affect the operations of other departments and links in the supply chain, however. Procurement managers may not have the authority to impose systems, procedures, standards or controls, but may have the *influence* (by virtue of their specialist expertise) to recommend them, and advise on their design and implementation.

Compliance

1.4 Law and regulation places certain requirements on products and services which may need to be taken into account in procurement decision-making and controls. Here are some examples.

- Quality standards and tolerances required to be *accredited* by various international quality standards
- Quality standards and tolerances required for *product safety*, under health and safety and consumer protection legislation and industry codes of practice (eg the strength, flexibility or weight-bearing capacity of construction materials; the chemical composition of materials to avoid health hazards; the restriction of ingredients such as additives in food products)
- Controls on the use, storage and transport of *substances and materials* which may be dangerous to health (eg chemicals, poisons, lead paint, asbestos, flammable or explosive materials, corrosive materials such as acids).
- *Environmental protection* law and regulation, dealing with issues such as the safe disposal or recyclability of waste and end-of-life products (including electrical and electronic waste and batteries)

1.5 Suppliers should be expected to be knowledgeable about, and compliant with, legislation relevant to their industry and products. However, the buyer is still liable in law if he incorporates outlawed materials or components in his products. One high-profile recent case study is the problems encountered by global toy company Mattel, which was forced to recall millions of toys, manufactured under licence in China, because the contractors had purchased paint contaminated with US/EU-banned levels of lead, from unauthorised suppliers.

1.6 Procurement professionals should therefore take proactive steps to:

- Draw specification teams' attention to known legal requirements
- Draw suppliers' attention to known legal requirements – especially if the law in the suppliers' country of operation is different from that of the buyer's
- Implement their own compliance checks (audits, monitoring and inspection) on suppliers and supplies
- Use suppliers which are certified under quality and environmental standards, or encourage favoured suppliers to become so certified.

Delegation to 'part-time' purchasers

1.7 In most organisations, a number of procurement activities will be undertaken by people who are not members of the procurement function or profession, and whose main activities are nothing to do with procurement.

- Part-time purchasing predates the introduction of a dedicated procurement function in many organisations, and user departments may have developed their own supplier contacts and 'ways of doing things'.
- User or budget-holder departments may believe themselves best qualified to make procurement decisions that affect their operations – particularly where items are very technical in nature, and users do not trust the procurement function to have sufficient specialist knowledge.
- Users may deliberately keep spending decisions away from the procurement department: a phenomenon sometimes known as 'maverick buying'. They may wish to control their own external expenditure, or may have a conflicting agenda (especially if procurement's priority is perceived to be cost or variety reduction, say).

1.8 There are some obvious disadvantages associated with part-time purchasing – as the phrase 'maverick buying' may suggest.

- Procurement decisions may be made unwisely, or processes carried out inefficiently, without the use of procurement expertise, disciplines and systems.
- User buyers may be too preoccupied with their main role to give sufficient attention to procurement procedures and decisions.
- It may be difficult to budget and control external spend if responsibilities for procurement are spread throughout the organisation.
- Unco-ordinated specifications and procurements by users, according to their own needs, typically lead to inefficiencies such as stock proliferation and over-specification (where procurement might challenge specifications, recommend generic or stocked items, and pursue standardisation or variety reduction).

1.9 However, there are also potential advantages to the devolution of procurement activities to part-time purchasers.

- Delegating responsibility for routine, low-value purchases frees up time for procurement specialists to devote to more complex and strategic tasks.
- Users may have technical skills and knowledge that need to be harnessed (eg for the development of effective specifications and service level agreements).
- The procurement function should be concerned to communicate good practice procurement disciplines as far as possible throughout the organisation – and devolved procurement may be a positive means to this end (if maverick buying can be controlled eg through approved supplier lists, checks and approvals).

Delegated authority for procurement

1.10 Defined levels and limits to delegated authority are vital to the governance of procurement, especially where procurement activities are decentralised. In the public sector, in particular, best practice requires a clear 'Scheme of Delegation' for procurement activity, setting out the minimum level of authorisation for each category of procurement in different value ranges. A typical example is given in Table 6.1

Table 6.1 *Scheme of delegation for a procurement organisation*

TYPE OF TRANSACTION	VALUE	CATEGORY	PROCEDURE	AUTHORISER
Low value	<$1k	Goods/Services/Works	Single verbal or written quotation	Local officer
	<$5k	Goods/Services	Single written quotation	Local officer
	<$10k	Works	Single written quotation	Local officer
Intermediate value	$5k–$50k	Goods/Services	Three written quotations	Section manager
	$10k–$50k	Works	Three written quotations	Section manager
High value	$50k	Goods/Services/Works	Sealed tender	Department head
	Over $50k	Goods/Services/Works	Full tender exercise	Procurement Unit

1.11 The most common sources of information on levels of approval for procurement, and means of obtaining the authority to proceed, are to be found in 'Standing Orders', 'Finance Manuals' or 'Procurement Manuals'. In addition to general delegation levels for procurement, such documents will also typically include rules and instructions for standard best practice procedures (eg the opening of tenders and key stages of contract approval).

Authorisations and sign-offs

1.12 Buyers spend huge sums of money, often a very large proportion of the total earned by the organisations that employ them. It is vital to ensure that the organisation receives full value for the sums spent – and that funds are not mismanaged, misused or misappropriated. To a large extent this is achieved by reliance on the ethical and technical standards of procurement professionals, but the principles of sound governance also require a defined system of checks and controls.

1.13 Authorisations or sign-offs may be required at a number of stages of the procurement process.

- When a **requisition** is originated in a user department, it must be signed by an authorised individual before being passed to procurement. This gives procurement the assurance they need that the requisition is for an item that is genuinely needed, and that the expenditure has been approved by the budget-holder.
- Before a **specification** is released to a supplier, it must have the formal approval of the procurement officer and ideally the prior certification of the supplier. This reduces the common risk of changes being made in order to solve problems not envisaged at the time the specification was finalised. This precaution should then be followed up by ensuring that any changes which are deemed necessary are subjected to appropriate approval procedures and documented in writing.
- When the **purchase order** is completed, it must be signed by an authorised person within the procurement department. The person signing it will usually do so with sight of the requisition and any other relevant documentation – and in the light of sourcing policies such as the use of preferred or approved suppliers lists, or the use of call-off contracts where available.
- When the supplier's **invoice** is received, it should not be passed for payment to the accounts department until procurement staff have carried out verification checks on goods inwards records, the purchase order or contract and so on. (We discuss this in more detail a bit later.)
- **Contract changes** must be authorised by the relevant contract manager, in order to ensure

that uncontrolled variations do not spring up, resulting in multiple versions, uncertainties and subsequent disputes.

Invoice clearance and payment

1.14 When an invoice or request for payment is received from a supplier, the buyer should check that it corresponds to the order or contract (in regard to the agreed price and payment terms) and to the goods received note (in regard to items actually received), and then *either* query discrepancies with the supplier *or* authorise the invoice for payment and pass it to the accounts department for payment.

1.15 Invoices should be paid within the period stated in the agreed terms of trade: often 30, 60 or 90 days. There may be defined policies (in addition to general ethical principles) about paying supplier invoices on time, as agreed.

2 Running competitions between suppliers

Competition

2.1 One area in which an organisation may have policy and procedure frameworks is the question of when, or in what circumstances, procurements must be subject to competition. For example, there may be strict policies for:

- How many quotations must be obtained, from different suppliers, for orders or contracts of different values
- When, or at what value threshold, procurements must be put up for competitive tender, or subjected to a competitive bidding process.

2.2 An organisation may have different procedures in place for orders of different volume or value.

- For order values under $100, say, there may be no formal requirement for supplier selection (although the policy might require the use of purchase cards or e-procurement systems, or referral of the requirement to the procurement function for consolidation, in order to minimise unnecessary transaction costs).
- For orders between $100 and $5,000, there may be a negotiation process (perhaps with preference given to approved or preferred suppliers), or a minimum of three suppliers may be requested to provide quotations, to ensure competitive pricing and value for money.
- For orders over $5,000 in value, a full competitive bidding or tendering process may be required. This means that buyers invite a number of suppliers to submit a tender (a bid) to supply the requirement. The buyer then evaluates all tenders received and awards the contract to the best supplier.

2.3 Standing Orders or Procurement Procedures Manuals may also provide for the authorisation of exceptional cases where it has not been possible to follow 'usual policy' (eg to obtain three written quotations for a procurement). They should nominate a manager of suitable rank, who may authorise exceptions to the rule, if there are reasonable grounds for them. The reason should be formally documented and recorded on file with the appropriate authorisations. This is important to create an 'audit trail', where decisions may be subject to internal and/or external scrutiny at a later date – as is particularly the case in the public sector.

2.4 These points are aspects of the 'competition role' of procurement and supply: topic 2.2 of the indicative content for this unit.

Different approaches to contract award

2.5 A buyer's requirements can be signalled to pre-qualified or approved suppliers in various ways, depending on the type of purchase and company policy.

2.6 The organisation may already have negotiated a **framework agreement** or standing contract with a supplier, to meet a requirement of a certain type. In such a case, the requirement will simply be notified by purchase or call-off order, on the pre-agreed terms.

2.7 There may be only one available supplier, or the organisation may have negotiated a preferred supplier or sole supplier agreement with a dependable supply partner. In such a case, the buyer may simply negotiate a contract with the preferred or designated supplier.

2.8 The organisation may send an 'enquiry' to one or more shortlisted suppliers, also called a **request for quotation** (RFQ). The RFQ will set out the details of the requirement: the contact details of the purchaser, the date and requisition reference, the quantity and description of goods or services required, the required place and date of delivery, and the buyer's standard terms and conditions of business. It will then invite the supplier(s) to submit a proposal and price for the job. These may be evaluated:

- On a competitive basis: eg the best value bid or quotation 'wins' the contract (as in competitive bidding or tendering)
- As a basis for negotiation with a preferred supplier. (Note, however, that it is not ethical practice to solicit quotations from more than one supplier if you have already decided where the contract will be awarded – eg just to 'motivate' a preferred supplier.)

3 Auditing compliance with internal procedures

3.1 The variety of decisions facing the procurement function is vast. Here are some of the issues they may address.

- Make/do internally or source from outside?
- Sourcing policy: single or multiple sourcing, or a combination depending on the materials concerned?
- Local or international sourcing?
- Centralise or decentralise purchasing decisions, or a combination of both, depending on materials, organisation structure and available information systems?
- What kind of systems to capture, analyse and share purchasing information?
- How to ensure compliance with relevant law, regulation and policy?
- What key performance indicators (KPIs), standards, targets and schedules will be used to measure and manage performance?
- What resources (including staff and skills) will be required to achieve objectives?

3.2 A purchasing management audit is 'a comprehensive, systematic, independent and periodic examination of a company's purchasing environment, objectives and tactics to identify problems and opportunities and to facilitate the development of appropriate action plans' (Scheuing, *Purchasing Management*).

- Comprehensive: the audit should cover every aspect of purchasing
- Systematic: a standard set of questions should be developed and used
- Independent: purchasing personnel should not evaluate themselves

- Periodic audits: the greatest value is achieved if the audit is performed periodically (eg annually), as this facilitates comparisons, checks and balances, and monitors progress

3.3 Purchasing management audits have four main organisational purposes.

- To verify the extent to which purchasing policies (including sustainable procurement) are being adhered to
- To ensure that procedures and methods conform to best working practice
- To monitor and measure the extent to which resources are used efficiently and effectively
- To assist in the detection of fraud.

3.4 It is important for purchasing performance to be measured, in order to:

- Motivate purchasing staff to maintain and improve performance and internal customer service
- Manage supply risk, by ensuring the ongoing control of quality, delivery, value and continuity of supply
- Ensure that purchasing is accountable for its part in achieving corporate objectives, and in satisfying the needs of key stakeholders (from whom feedback should be gathered as part of the process)
- Support two-way or joint performance measurement and problem-solving with key suppliers, as part of their partnership in achieving results and improvements
- Provide feedback for contribution and achievement recognition (enhancing staff morale and purchasing status and credibility)
- Provide feedback for learning, continuous improvement of performance, and supply chain relationship development

3.5 *Johnson* argues that a range of performance measures may be used by managers.

- External measures such as: market share, customer satisfaction and/or loyalty, number of new customers, number and type of customer complaints.
- Operational measures such as: on-time in-full deliveries, number and type of errors and defects, utilisation of facilities and equipment, productivity, capacity (eg equipment and staff availability)
- Financial measures such as total costs and cost per customer, costs of labour, order processing, procurement and inventory, total revenue and revenue per customer, operating profit and profit per customer
- Development measures such as staff satisfaction, labour turnover, number of suggestions, improvements and innovations, training hours, involvement in quality teams.

3.6 Such measures will be focused on providing the 'quantitative or qualitative assessment of progress over a given time towards the achievement of corporate or operational goals and objectives relating to purchasing economies, efficiency and effectiveness' (Lysons & Farrington).

- *Economies* means minimising the cost of resources required, without loss of quality: in other words, achieving value for money, or 'spending less'.
- *Efficiency* means maximising the output of goods or services for the resources used to produce them: in other words, achieving productivity, or 'spending well'.
- *Effectiveness* means the extent to which the actual results of activities and projects match the intended results: in other words, achieving objectives, or 'spending wisely'.

3.7 Arjen Van Weele points out that different performance measures will be used, depending on the role of the purchasing function in the organisation. If its role is perceived as primarily administrative, measures such as lead times, productivity and error rates may be used. If its role is primarily commercial, cost savings will be a priority. At a more strategic level, from a supply chain perspective, emphasis will shift to higher measures such as strategic alignment, relationship management, supplier leverage and so on.

Chapter summary

- Purchasers have a duty to comply with law, regulations and standards relevant to their activities.
- There are various reasons why part-time purchasing takes place in organisations. Mostly this is to be discouraged, but it does have some advantages.
- Most procurement departments will operate a 'hierarchy' of approvals, meaning that lower-value procurements will need a lower level of authorisation than high-value purchases.
- Procurement staff run competitions between suppliers to obtain the best possible trading terms.
- It is important to audit compliance with internal procedures. A purchasing management audit is a systematic approach to doing this.

Self-test questions

Numbers in brackets refer to the paragraphs where you can check your answers.

1 List areas in which purchasing policies and procedures will typically need to be formulated. (1.2)

2 List areas in which procurement staff will need to comply with external regulations. (1.4)

3 List advantages and disadvantages of part-time purchasing. (1.8, 1.9)

4 At what stages of the procurement process may authorisation and sign-off be required? (1.13)

5 What is a request for quotation? (2.8)

6 What are the purposes of a purchasing management audit? (3.3)

7 List possible performance measures for evaluating purchasing performance. (3.5)

CHAPTER 7

Key Economic Sectors

Assessment criteria and indicative content

3.1 Identify the main economic sectors that impact on a procurement and supply function

- Primary, secondary and tertiary sectors

Section headings

1 Introduction
2 The primary sector
3 The secondary sector
4 The tertiary sector
5 The retail sector

1 Introduction

1.1 It is common to distinguish between three major industry sectors, according to the type of process they perform.

- *Primary industries* are concerned with extracting natural resources or producing raw materials. This sector includes oil and mineral extraction (mining), agriculture and forestry.
- *Secondary industries* are engaged in transforming raw materials into end components, assemblies or finished products. This sector includes the manufacturing, engineering and construction industries, for example.
- *Tertiary industries* are those engaged in the development and provision of services. This sector includes professional services, financial services, transport, hospitality and so on.

1.2 Sectors are simply ways of grouping organisations. Economic sectors are grouped by ownership: public or private. Industry sectors may be grouped by industry type (resource extraction, production or service provision), area of activity (eg retail, manufacturing, construction, media and publishing and so on), size (eg the small business sector) or primary objective (profit-making or non-profit-making).

1.3 This classification is neither clear cut nor exhaustive. Agriculture these days has some of the features of secondary industry, for example, and is often classified as such. The retail, energy and IT sectors do not fit clearly into any one category and are sometimes regarded as sectors in their own right. Nor is it helpful to separate the three types of activity when thinking about supply chains. The purchasing function in a manufacturing organisation, say, might have to buy across a number of categories: raw materials, manufactured goods (such as components, or computers, tools, machinery and office furniture) and services (such as IT consultancy, insurance and transport).

1.4 It should not be surprising, however, to find that purchasing priorities and practices do differ from one sector to another. Clearly, the organisational characteristics and operational challenges of an oil drilling company are likely to be very different from those of a management consultancy – and these differences are likely to be apparent at least to some extent within the purchasing function.

2 The primary sector

2.1 In a primary sector industry such as mining the following important characteristics may be identified.

- The purchasing spend is very high. This is above all because large, specialised, heavy-duty machinery is often necessary, and because expenditure on spares and tools is a significant element.
- Stock levels are typically high and materials management activities should be planned so as to control the costs of stockholding.
- The specialised nature of most supplies, as well as their high value in many cases, mean that most purchases are routed through a specialist purchasing department, rather than being processed in an *ad hoc* way by operational staff. This enables a good level of control and means that the benefits of professional purchasing expertise are realised.
- Partly as a consequence of the above, it is common to find that purchasing is represented at a senior level in the organisation, possibly on the main board.
- The nature of operations is very different from a continuous manufacturing environment. In particular, the problems of links between one stage and the next in a continuous production line are less urgent, and techniques such as just in time and materials requirements planning are less relevant.
- Another aspect of this theme is the nature of the supplier base. The value of items purchased on a regular basis is proportionately less than in a manufacturing firm, while the value of special purchases is proportionately higher. This can mean that the supplier base changes more often and more rapidly than is common for manufacturing companies.

Supplying to and purchasing for primary industries

2.2 One of the problems peculiar to the primary sector is that managers have no choice in where they locate their operating facilities. No doubt it would be easier to build an oil rig inland than in the middle of the North Sea; but since the oil is in fact situated in the latter location the easy option is not available.

2.3 Similarly, a quarrying company must operate where supplies of, say, slate actually exist in the ground. This may well mean operating half way up a mountain.

2.4 Clearly this makes the provision of the right supplies in the right place at the right time all the more difficult. Purchasing staff must consider:

- how to arrange transport of the materials to the remote location
- how to optimise order quantities bearing in mind the additional logistical problems involved
- how to store materials once they are in place
- the additional costs that all this gives rise to.

2.5 The same problems impact on suppliers. Suppliers must not only undertake a more difficult task in the actual delivery of materials, but also have less margin for error in both quality and delivery performance. This is because if materials are found to be defective or unsuitable the problem of replacement will be more complex than in the usual case.

2.6 Similarly, a supplier of, say, capital equipment will normally provide support and service operations. In the case of an extractive industry the problems that this leads to are magnified. For one thing, the equipment involved is often of a very large scale, implying that support and service requirements are correspondingly larger. For another, the difficulties of access can pose problems in relation to speed of response and cost.

2.7 The buyer's role in managing these problems is a crucial one. From the beginning, his task is to liaise closely with suppliers in anticipating the difficulties and devising solutions. He needs to ensure that suppliers are fully aware of the particular problems that may apply and of their obligations in overcoming them.

2.8 One step that will usually be taken to minimise these problems is the provision of emergency and standby materials, invariably in larger quantities than would be necessary for a manufacturing operation of similar size. This of course runs counter to modern ideas on stock minimisation but the particular circumstances of the primary industry sector demand it.

2.9 Once again, the expertise of the purchasing professional is vital. Drawing on experience of historical usage patterns the professional buyer is able to determine a level of emergency and standby materials that balances operational requirements with cost considerations.

3 The secondary sector

The manufacturing sector

3.1 This sector used to be overwhelmingly the largest economic sector in most developed economies, and remains hugely important for prosperity, despite the fact that service industries now account for a larger slice of the economic cake. The purchasing literature reflects the fact that very many buyers are employed in manufacturing companies. By implication or explicitly much of the discussion in this text and the standard purchasing literature is based on a manufacturing and engineering background.

3.2 The essence of this sector is that the manufacturer takes a series of inputs from earlier stages in the supply chain and performs operations upon them to create a finished product. The inputs may include raw materials, components, and subassemblies. The manufacturer applies resources (manpower, machinery etc) to convert these into the final output for sale to his customers.

3.3 A few of the distinguishing characteristics of manufacturing companies, as they relate to purchasing, are singled out below, but you should bear in mind that most of what you read in the literature is relevant to this sector.

- Purchasing is a relatively advanced function in many manufacturing companies. Often purchasing staff have strategic responsibilities in addition to their operational duties.
- Partly this has come about through the transformation of manufacturing operations in recent decades. World class techniques such as just in time, total quality management, and materials requirements planning have caused a re-evaluation of the role of supply chain management with a consequent upgrading in the status of purchasing. Representation of the function at main board level is common.
- Purchasing's key internal customer is the production function. The most important task is to ensure that production teams have materials of the right quality available in the right place at the right time in the right quantity, achieving all this at the right price – the traditional **five rights of purchasing**.

- The value of materials which are bought on a regular basis is a high proportion of total purchasing spend. To achieve the 'five rights' for such materials purchasing strategy has focused on a slim supplier base with close relations between buyer and supplier.
- The role of the purchasing professional typically extends through almost the whole spectrum of organisational activities, beginning with new product development right through to delivery to customers.

Manufacturing supply chains

3.4 Key characteristics of manufacturing which impact on supply chains include the following.

- The introduction of world class techniques such as just in time, total quality management and materials requirements planning has extended the integration of supply networks and the role of supply chain management.
- Operations management is the focal point of the supply chain (and the key internal customer of purchasing).
- The value of materials bought on a regular basis is likely to be a high proportion of total purchasing spend. Strategies therefore typically focus on a slim supplier base, with close relations between buyers and suppliers (particularly for strategic items).
- Accurate demand forecasting is vital to avoid over-production (with possible waste) or under-production (with possible customer dissatisfaction).
- The effective management of quality issues throughout the supply chain is essential to ensure a steady flow of consistently high-quality output.

3.5 Several writers have noted that the structure and priorities of the supply chain will depend to a large extent on the complexity of the product manufactured and the level of uncertainty and dynamism in its environment.

- For complex goods in dynamic environments (eg capital intensive industries such as aerospace, shipbuilding and construction), quality management and supply chain agility are a priority. For complex goods in stable environments (eg consumer durables or automotive), value for money and demand-driven supply may be a priority.
- For simple goods in dynamic environments (eg fashion, cosmetics, food and drink), short cycle times may be key, in response to short product lifecycles. And for simple goods in stable environments (eg commodities), process efficiency and cost improvement are key, in response to price sensitivity.

The FMCG sector (secondary)

3.6 Fast moving consumer goods (FMCG) products include confectionery, toiletries, soft drinks, mass fashion items and so on. The FMCG sector is a special example of the manufacturing sector, with focus on production of goods for consumer mass markets. The FMCG manufacturer depends for his success on volume sales.

3.7 Competitive forces in this sector are very strong, with numerous manufacturers attempting to push their products to a position of market leadership. This has led to a vast proliferation of choice for the consumer. Just check out the number of different brands of toothpaste, for example, on display in a typical supermarket.

3.8 One implication of this is the crucial importance of branding. Faced with many competing products, consumers are reassured by recognising familiar brands. Often, brand loyalty is their main reason for selecting one manufacturer's product rather than another's. Purchasers in this industry can expect to be spending large amounts of money on promoting brand awareness, eg by means of media advertising.

3.9 Another feature of this sector is a very short product lifecycle. Although many brands have stood the test of time (albeit with many changes to their basic specifications over the years), there are intense competitive pressures to introduce new products constantly. This is so that manufacturers can respond to every nuance of customers' changing needs and so acquire and defend market share. Purchasers must be constantly alert to the need for different materials, ingredients, packaging etc in order to satisfy this need.

The engineering sector (secondary)

3.10 There are many different types of engineering firm.

- Civil engineers are engaged in the construction of roads, bridges, railways, buildings etc
- Mechanical engineers are engaged in the design and production of plant and equipment.
- Electrical engineers are engaged in the design and production of electrical and electronic goods.
- Chemical engineers are engaged in the design and production of chemicals and chemical processing plants.
- Software engineers are engaged in the design and development of software systems.

3.11 This list is not meant to be exhaustive, but gives an idea of the scope of engineering activities. All of these different types of engineer are engaged in design activities and will give high priority to protection of their intellectual property.

3.12 There are differences in the kind of work undertaken by engineering firms. Typically these firms will be involved in three main categories of operation.

- New build (eg construction of a road or a bridge, creation of a new software system)
- Renewals (eg major enhancements to an existing construction or project)
- Maintenance (ongoing care and repair of constructions and installations)

4 The tertiary sector

4.1 The tertiary sector refers to providers of intangible services (rather than tangible goods). As we saw earlier, the nature of service provision differs in important ways from the provision of tangible goods.

4.2 Perhaps the key point about service supply chains is the importance of people in delivering service and differentiating one service provider from another. Training, motivation, empowerment and cultural values are important factors in service supply. Supply chain management will also contribute to competitive advantage through cost efficiency and the integrated management of information.

4.3 The result is that in many service companies the purchasing function is relatively undeveloped. Indeed, it is sometimes found that many purchasing responsibilities are undertaken by non-purchasing personnel because a centralised purchasing function is either completely absent or ineffective.

4.4 Generalisations are always dangerous, but it is probably fair to say that in many service companies purchasing activities are dispersed throughout the organisation, rather than being under centralised control; and to the extent that a centralised function exists at all, its role is mainly clerical and administrative. This situation is changing as increased competition forces service companies to examine value added throughout their supply chains, but the stage of development is less advanced than in manufacturing organisations.

4.5 One characteristic that has retarded the development of purchasing functions in service companies is the absence of a clear link between inputs, processing and outputs. In the case of a manufacturing company this link is very clear: materials are bought in for $X, these are worked on at a cost of $Y and eventually converted into finished products for sale at $Z.

4.6 In a service company this process is much less clear, especially since the value of bought in materials is usually low as a percentage of sales output. For example, whereas a manufacturer might expect, say, 60 per cent of his sales revenue to be absorbed by the cost of bought out materials, for a service company the proportion might be as low as 10 per cent. Most of the inputs of many service companies consist of staff salaries, where purchasing expertise has little to contribute.

4.7 What items are bought out in a typical service organisation? This will obviously depend heavily on the exact nature of the organisation, but the following are likely answers.

- Office equipment and supplies such as stationery
- Computer hardware and software
- Motor vehicles
- Advertising and design services
- Maintenance services (for computers, vehicles and buildings)
- In some cases, capital goods (such as a provider of logistics services who must invest heavily in premises, materials handling equipment, heavy goods vehicles etc)

4.8 Whereas in a manufacturing company a purchasing manager's main 'customer' is the production function, in a service company hardly any of the buyer's effort is directed at 'production'. This is well illustrated by the list above. For this reason among others line managers in such companies have tended to think of purchasing purely as a support function and this has been a factor in the low priority accorded to purchasing expertise.

The growing influence of procurement in the services sector

4.9 However, a number of trends are beginning to alter this picture. One is the increased use of **outsourcing**. As service companies focus on core activities they are increasingly likely to outsource such support functions as security, catering, printing, and information technology. The logical conclusion to this development is the use of a facilities management approach under which all such activities are placed under the responsibility of a single facilities manager.

4.10 Another trend with important implications for purchasing is the increased size of service companies and the increased scale of their operations, often resulting from mergers and takeovers which reduce the number of companies operating in any particular sector. Once operations have reached a certain scale the desirability of defined purchasing responsibilities becomes more pressing.

4.11 This is clearer in companies where capital spending is relatively high. Because large sums of money are involved, the impetus to adopt appropriate purchasing techniques may well be present. Without this, the purchase of specialist capital equipment (eg computer hardware and systems) may be left to users whose priorities are not mainly directed to low cost. From their perspective, reliability and quality are vital, value for money less so.

4.12 More generally, it can be said that when responsibility for purchasing decisions is spread throughout an organisation, management lose the important 'value for money' perspective. End users of the items purchased are not trained to emphasise this criterion and may instead focus on a solution which has worked reliably in the past, without considering whether better or lower-cost solutions may now be available.

4.13 In all these instances the potential value of a strong purchasing function is clear. If purchasing expertise is directed only at routine low-cost items the scope for cost efficiencies is much reduced. By extending the scope of purchasing involvement senior managers can obtain cost benefits that may be vital in securing competitive advantage.

4.14 This sounds easy enough, but in practice difficulties are encountered. The first hurdle to overcome is at the level of senior managers. Unless they can be persuaded of the strategic importance of the issue any initiative from the purchasing department is likely to be stillborn.

4.15 Even with the support of senior management, there are obstacles that must be removed. Chief among these is the probable reluctance of operational managers to hand over purchasing responsibility. They may perceive purchasing staff as having different priorities from themselves, and may resist what they see as merely a cost cutting exercise. Purchasing must be able to convince them that, while cost is important, operational priorities (such as reliability and delivery lead time) will also be addressed with no less enthusiasm than in the past.

Service supply chains

4.16 In service organisations, the value of bought-in materials is generally a low proportion of sales output and total input: such organisations are highly labour-intensive. However, physical supply may be important if services are based on the use of physical or 'hard' assets: property (as in a hotel or bank branch), vehicles (as in a logistics company or airline) or machinery (as in a computer bureau or printing service). In addition, service organisations commonly buy in goods and services for their own use: office equipment and supplies, computer systems, vehicles, advertising and design services, maintenance services and so on.

4.17 Various trends can be observed in service supply chains.

- Services are increasingly about the management and supply of information: financial services, information and research, entertainment and transport bookings, consultancy, advertising and design and so on. Many information storage, query and processing functions have been automated – and can now be offered direct to the consumer through the internet, interactive kiosks, ATM machines and so on. Supply chains are thus shortening to direct interaction between the service provider and consumer, increasingly on a self-service basis.
- Information can replace inventory (eg in the case of Dell's assembled-to-order computers).
- Services are increasingly outsourced, as organisations focus on core activities and subcontract support functions such as security, catering, printing, IT, sales and customer service, fleet management, HR selection and training, logistics and facilities management.
- The combination of automation and outsourcing has enabled the development of virtual service organisations and networks. Financial services are a good example: mortgages, insurance and investment products are often supplied by a network of providers, drawn on by brokers who interface with consumers.

5 The retail sector

5.1 In this section we look at the work of buyers employed by wholesalers and retailers. The task of such buyers is to purchase goods which will then be sold onwards to customers with little or no work having been done to them in the meantime. This contrasts with a manufacturing environment, in which buyers purchase materials that will be converted into finished products.

5.2 It should be obvious that important principles of purchasing are as relevant here as they are in manufacturing environments. For example, modern approaches to quality assurance, stock control and supplier relations remain vital. Even so, the nature of the work is different in important respects, and the objective here is to isolate these differences and discuss their impact for buyers.

5.3 The most crucial difference is that buyers in resale environments are usually much closer to their (external) customers than is common in manufacturing. This is because the decision on what to buy is crucially related to expectations of what will sell. There is pressure on buyers in this sector to find new lines that will entice additional customers and generate additional income. This is very different from the situation in manufacturing and suggests that an important part of the buyer's training should be in marketing and selling.

5.4 The importance of these distinctions should not be exaggerated. For one thing, the similarities between purchasing activities in different sectors probably always outweigh the specific differences. Some specific differences are being eroded as purchasing disciplines evolve towards a world class standard.

5.5 An example of this is the question of supplier relations. As Arjen Van Weele points out, these have typically been less durable in resale than in manufacturing. However, there is a definite trend towards closer and more lasting relationships. One way in which this is evidenced is in the closer involvement of some retailers in the production procedures of manufacturers.

5.6 Partly this is a matter of quality assurance. A retailer wishes to be able to talk with confidence to his customers about the quality of the goods he offers for sale. This is best achieved by working closely with his suppliers, and this implies long-term relations.

5.7 Partly also it reflects the situation where the distinction between supplier and retailer is vague, as has historically been the case with Marks & Spencer. Marks & Spencer sell their own branded items and their suppliers act, in effect, as the manufacturing arm of the company. For this reason, it is very well known that particularly close relations have existed between M&S and their suppliers. Baily, Farmer, Jessop and Jones (in *Purchasing Principles and Management*) state that M&S have sometimes been called 'a manufacturer without factories'.

5.8 Where an organisation sells 'own-label' products, the role of the retail buyer becomes much more similar to that of the industrial buyer; in each case, purchasing aims to get from the supplier a product which matches the buyer's specification.

5.9 Often a producer will produce both their own branded goods (for sale at a premium price) and equivalent non-branded goods (sometimes referred to as **white label goods**). These latter will be sold to supermarkets who want to apply their own branding. From the producer's point of view, this maximises revenue by satisfying all sectors of the market. The discounted price is affordable to the supplier because the white label version will usually be of lower quality and cheaper to produce.

5.10 A number of issues are increasingly subject to debate among buyers and suppliers.

- Buyers may seek to encourage standardisation and variety reduction among manufacturers.
- Buyers may put pressure on manufacturers to provide training to personnel handling their goods.
- Buyers may look to suppliers for a contribution to advertising costs to the extent that this is likely to benefit the supplier.

5.11 Technological developments have left few areas of business untouched, but their impact on retailing has been particularly dramatic. Improvements in production technology have led to shorter product lifecycles (ie more rapid introduction of new products) which places increased burdens on the retail buyer to stay abreast of events. One step to this end has been greater involvement of buyers in the product development process.

5.12 Purchase ordering is streamlined to suit the fast turnover that is common in resale organisations. Frequent deliveries are essential, which means that ordering procedures must be simple and rapid. Invariably, advanced information technology is used, including electronic data interchange linking buyers' ordering systems to suppliers' sales systems.

5.13 Once goods are delivered to retail outlets or distribution centres they are recorded in the inventory control system. Many retailers have highly automated systems under which suppliers' performance levels are evaluated at this point in relation to on-time delivery and quality.

5.14 Another important aspect of information technology is the facility it gives to obtain and analyse information about buying patterns among consumers, especially by the use of EPOS systems (electronic point of sale). This is vital for marketing staff in planning prices and promotions and in assessing potential demand for new products. Equally, it gives important clues to buyers as to which products are likely to sell and therefore which products should be bought.

The role of the retail buyer

5.15 The above discussion should have made it clear that buyers in the retail sector may become involved in many different aspects of the business, some of them not conventionally regarded as part of the purchasing function at all.

5.16 For example, buyers may become involved in market research activity, partly to establish what their customers wish to buy but also to monitor the activities of competitors. Statistics provided by suppliers are an important source of this kind of information, but should be treated with caution: suppliers have a vested interest in presenting a picture that will promote sales of their products.

5.17 Buyers should also be involved in the process of setting expenditure budgets. This process involves every layer of an organisation, from the very top down to the lowest levels of managerial control. Within a framework laid down by overall organisational budgets individual buyers must negotiate their own spending limits, and other targets such as sales volume and profit margin to be achieved on particular products for which they are responsible.

5.18 Clearly a major part of the buyer's role is in the selection of products and suppliers. Co-operation with other functional areas such as marketing and merchandising is important in this field. Key decision variables obviously include purchase cost (including discounts and trade credit), but buyers will also be influenced by reliability of supply, the extent to which suppliers invest in new product development, and the level of marketing support given. Marketing support could range from high-profile advertising by the manufacturer to provision of ready-to-sell packaging for point of sale promotional material.

5.19 Buyers are also involved in the management of physical inventory, including storage and distribution. It may or may not be appropriate to use the buying firm's own storage facilities. Often in retail contexts it is **not** appropriate, and a mix of just in time principles and storage at suppliers' premises enables buyers to minimise stock held.

5.20 As already explained, an important part of buying is selling! This is the test of whether the buyer has bought well, and the buyer has an obvious interest in becoming involved in this area.

5.21 A common example is the involvement of buyers in sales promotions; where promotions take place the buyer must be alert to the need for additional ordering to meet the expected increase in demand. For consumers, it is frustrating and a source of ill feeling towards the supplier and stockist if a product advertised and promoted strongly is not available for purchase.

5.22 Buyers are involved in monitoring the sales performance of their products. In many retail organisations the responsibilities of buyers include a certain amount of direct communication with suppliers. In other cases, the centralised nature of the purchasing function makes such communication less feasible. However this may be, it is clearly essential that a buyer monitors sales figures produced by the information system.

5.23 Finally, buyers must be concerned with evaluation of suppliers. Often they will be aided by computer-produced statistics relating to quality and on-time delivery.

Retail supply chains

5.24 The distinctive feature of retail supply chains is the direct relationship between the retailer and the final consumer. Buyers have to identify new lines that will entice additional customers and demand – which requires marketing-oriented competencies in addition to purchasing competencies. Supply chain management will be focused on securing the timely availability or fulfilment of a wide variety of products in response to customer demand.

5.25 Various forms of collaboration have been an increasing feature of retail buyer-supplier relationships, including training of retail sales and service staff by manufacturers, and supplier contribution to retailers' advertising and display costs (where this is of benefit to the supplier). Technological integration has also become widespread, in the form of EDI purchasing (electronic data interchange – transferring data automatically between buyer's and supplier's computer systems), automated inventory control and replenishment, and demand management via electronic point of sale (EPOS) systems.

Chapter summary

- It is common to distinguish between primary, secondary and tertiary industry sectors.
- In the primary sector, many problems arise for procurement from the fact that locations may be remote.
- In the secondary sector, procurement is long established and arguably better developed than in other sectors.
- Specific areas of the secondary sector include FMCG and engineering works.
- The tertiary sector is very labour intensive, with less emphasis on goods purchased from outside suppliers. Despite this, procurement is coming to be seen as a vital discipline even in this sector.
- In the retail sector, a key feature is the link between purchases and sales. Buyers must be skilled at identifying items that can be sold onwards to customers.

Self-test questions

Numbers in brackets refer to the paragraphs where you can check your answers.

1 Distinguish between primary, secondary and tertiary industries. (1.1)

2 List distinguishing characteristics of primary industries. (2.1)

3 What problems may be caused by the remote locations of primary industries? (2.4)

4 List distinguishing characteristics of manufacturing industries. (3.3)

5 Give examples of fast moving consumer goods. (3.6)

6 Why is the procurement function often undeveloped in service companies? (4.3)

7 What factors are leading to a greater development of procurement in service companies? (4.9ff)

8 What are white label goods? (5.9)

9 Suggest aspects of the buyer's role in retail organisations. (5.15ff)

CHAPTER 8

Demand and Supply

Assessment criteria and indicative content

3.2 Describe the impact of demand and supply on markets

- Demand and supply curves
- How demand and supply factors can change
- How demand and supply factors can impact on pricing and availability

Section headings

1 Micro economics
2 Demand and supply curves
3 How demand and supply factors can change
4 Pricing and availability

1 Micro economics

Defining micro economics

1.1 Micro economics is the study of how firms and individuals make decisions to allocate limited resources. In principle, there is no limit to the demand for goods and services: people and firms always want more. But there is a limit to their power of acquiring goods and services. This is because they must provide resources in exchange, and the available resources are always finite.

1.2 In studying micro economics we are looking at how firms behave in the markets they operate in: what goods they decide to produce, in what quantities, at what cost, and for what selling prices.

1.3 This is in contrast to macro economics, which is the study of overall economic activity, not the study of individuals and firms. Macro economics is concerned with 'big picture' issues such as economic growth or decline, inflation, unemployment and so on.

What is a market?

1.4 A market is a place where buyers and sellers of a product are brought together to trade. This may be a physical location where they interact face to face (like a supermarket or car showroom) – but it may equally well be 'cyber space' (as in online share trading, online stores and auction sites such as e-Bay) or a network of contacts with intermediaries (eg share brokers or export agencies) so that buyer and seller never deal directly with each other. In each case, the main features of a market are the exchange of goods or services and payment in some form.

1.5 **Product markets** are the markets in which a firm sells its products and services to consumers. **Supply (or factor) markets** are the markets in which a firm purchases the resources it needs for production (eg materials and labour). The purchasing function therefore deals primarily in various supply markets.

1.6 As we saw in an earlier chapter, a **market economy** (or **free market system**) is one in which basic economic choices (what to produce, how, for whom and at what price) are made through the market – by consumer choice – without state intervention. To understand how these choices are made you need to be familiar with a key economic concept: the market mechanism. This is the relationship between demand and supply for a particular product or service, and the way in which price affects both.

2 Demand and supply curves

The market mechanism: demand and supply

2.1 *Demand* is the quantity of goods that consumers are willing and able to buy. It varies with price: in general, as the price of a good goes up, demand goes down – because some people will cut down on their purchases, or switch to cheaper substitutes.

2.2 However, this is a simplified picture, because other factors than price also impact on demand for products. We will return to this point later in the chapter.

2.3 It may help to see a very basic diagram of the relationship between price and demand, called a 'demand curve'. As prices rise, demand falls, as shown by a movement *along* the downward demand curve: Figure 8.1 (a). However, changes in the other determining factors lead to a *shift of the demand curve itself:* at *any* given price, demand may fall or rise: Figure 8.1 (b).

Figure 8.1 *The demand curve*

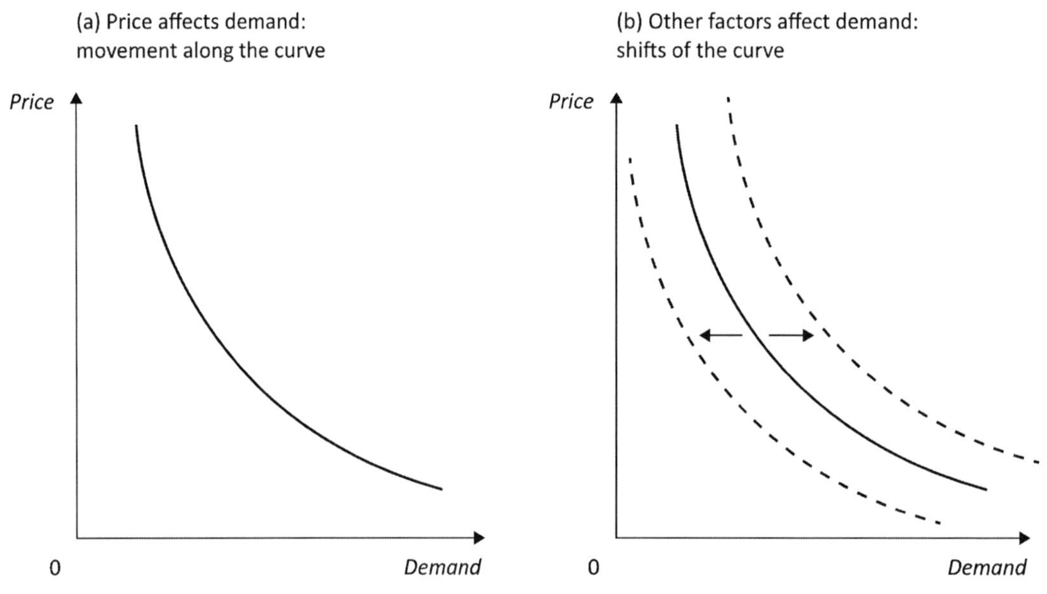

2.4 *Supply* is the amount that firms are willing and able to sell. This too varies with price: in general, as the market price of a good rises, supply also rises – because higher prices mean greater profitability, increasing the willingness of firms to produce more.

2.5 Once again, other factors than price can affect supply and we will return to this point later.

2.6 Again, it may help to see a very basic diagram of the relationship between price and quantity of supply, called a 'supply curve'. As prices rise, supply also rises, as shown by a movement *along* the upward supply curve: Figure 8.2 (a). However, changes in the other determining factors lead to a *shift of the supply curve itself:* at *any* given market price, producers may raise or lower supply: Figure 8.2 (b).

Figure 8.2 *The supply curve*

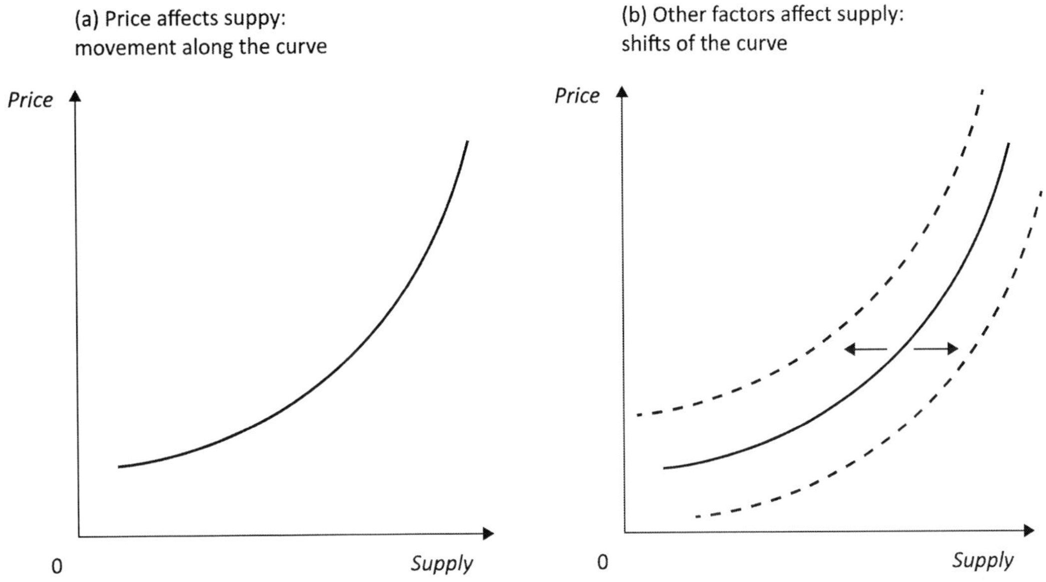

2.7 There is one price (called the **equilibrium price**) at which producers wish to sell the same amount as consumers wish to buy: in other words, the market 'clears' (without either surplus supply or unsatisfied demand).

2.8 Say that, at a certain price, supply exceeds demand. Goods will pile up in the shops – and the price will start to fall. Falling prices act as a signal to suppliers to cut back on supply – at the same time as increasing demand again. The market eventually stabilises at a price at which the supply of a good matches demand for that good: Figure 8.3. Both parties are relatively satisfied, so there is (for the moment) no need for further adjustment.

Figure 8.3 *Equilibrium price*

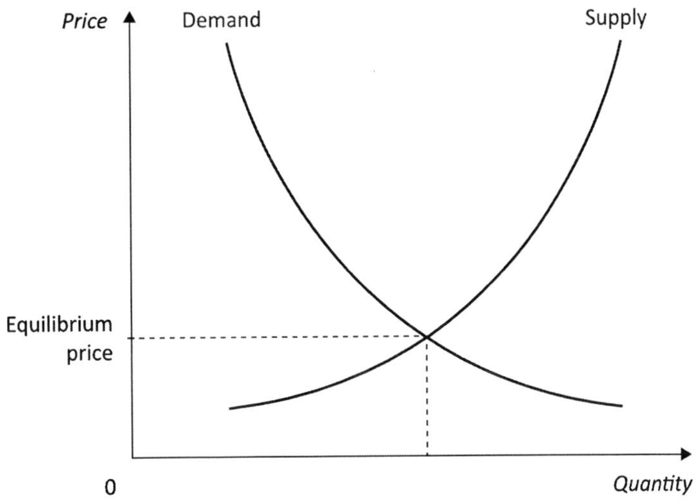

2.9 So by consuming a product at a given level at a given price, consumers are effectively determining the resources that will be devoted to production of that product. Price is the economy's mechanism for allocating resources.

3 How demand and supply factors can change

What determines the level of demand for a product?

3.1 Demand is the quantity of a good which consumers want, and are willing and able to pay for. If you think about how you decide which goods to buy, you will realise that there are many factors entering into the decision. The main influences on the demand for goods and services are discussed below.

3.2 **Price** is probably the most significant factor. The higher the price, the less likely people are to buy it. For a particular product, economists can create a **demand curve** – a graph indicating how demand falls as price rises. We saw an example of a demand curve earlier in the chapter.

3.3 In general, the more **income** people earn, the more they will buy. The demand for most goods increases as income rises.

3.4 Two or more goods are defined as **substitutes** if they are interchangeable (or almost interchangeable) in giving consumers utility. For example, margarine is a fairly close substitute for butter. If something has a substitute, you will probably compare the price of the substitute with the price of the good you are thinking of buying. Butter is more expensive than margarine, so, apart from the health considerations, you may decide to buy margarine. On the other hand, milk has very few substitutes, so your decision to buy it will not depend heavily on the price of other products.

3.5 Suppose the price of margarine rises. Even if it is still cheaper than butter, some people will decide that the difference in price is so small that they would rather buy butter. Demand for margarine will fall, while that for butter will rise.

3.6 Conversely, if the price of a substitute falls, then demand for the good in question will also fall, as people switch to the substitute.

3.7 If Good A and Good B are **substitutes**, a **rise** in the price of one will cause a **rise** in demand for the other, and *vice versa*.

3.8 **Complements** are goods which must be used together. For example, a compact disc player is no good without any compact discs. The price of a good's complements is very important when considering whether or not to buy it. You may be able to afford the player, but if you will not be able to buy any compact discs, there is little point in the purchase.

3.9 If the price of a **complement** rises, then demand for the good in question will **fall**. Conversely, if the price of a complement falls, demand for the good will rise.

3.10 **Taste** is influenced by many different things. You may decide not to buy butter purely on health grounds, having been made aware of its high cholesterol levels. Or fashion may induce you to buy a new pair of shoes even if you don't really need them and cannot afford them. Of all the factors influencing demand, taste is the most difficult one to quantify.

3.11 Clearly, the size of total demand depends on the number of people who are aware of the good's existence, who are able to obtain it and who are likely to want it. **Market size** can be altered by changes in the size and structures of the population. If the birth rate falls in an area, this will have a long-term effect on the total population size and will have a more immediate effect in reducing the number of babies, hence influencing the demand for prams, equipment and clothing designed for babies. It will, of course, also affect the demand for school places, for schoolteachers and for people to train teachers.

3.12 It is not only the volume and quality of **advertising** that can influence demand for a product but also the amount of advertising in comparison with that for competing products. Advertisers cannot often increase total consumption; more often they transfer it from one good to another.

3.13 A change in the **quality** of goods or services will have an effect on how much will be demanded at a particular price. An improvement in quality will increase demand.

What determines the level of supply of a product?

3.14 **Supply** is the quantity of a good which suppliers (or a single supplier) are willing and able to produce in a given period. As with demand, the decision about how much to supply depends on many factors, of which one of the most important is price. In the suppliers' case, the cost of production is also of paramount importance.

3.15 The higher the market **price** of the product, the more the supplier will wish to supply because he will make a bigger profit. For a particular product, economists can create a **supply curve** – a graph indicating how supply increases as price rises.

3.16 In producing goods for sale, the supplier will incur **costs**. Clearly, these must be covered if the supplier is to stay in business. The supplier will therefore compare the market price with his costs to make sure that production will be profitable. Costs will change over time, as technology and production methods change.

3.17 Certain industries are particularly susceptible to **uncontrollable factors**, such as changes in the weather. The most obvious example is agriculture, where bad weather can diminish or even obliterate supply. If the farmer is lucky he can smooth out some of the fluctuations by storing produce during good times and releasing his stocks during bad times, but not all goods can be stored.

3.18 **The level of technology** influences the efficiency with which capital or machines and labour can be used to produce goods. Improved technology enables firms to produce more with a given input of resources, ie at the same cost, and can thus be expected to increase the amount that they are willing to supply at given prices.

3.19 Advanced technology may not be worthwhile in some forms of production unless a certain minimum level of production is desired by customers. Firms may not, therefore, be willing to supply at all unless this level is reached. Alternatively, they may only be willing to supply at high prices because at low quantity levels they have to use expensive methods of production. There may then be two sets of supply conditions – one for low production levels at expensive production costs and one for high levels of production where advanced technology can be employed to reduce the production cost per unit.

3.20 **New entrants** to the supply market increase the supply of goods or services in that market.

3.21 The availability of **complements** is also important. Many goods are linked to each other – for example, cameras and films. A reduction in the price of cameras will mean that more cameras are supplied (at a lower price); this increase in demand will have a knock-on effect on the supply of films without any change in their price.

Shifts in demand and supply

3.22 Figure 8.1(a) shows how price and demand are related. As price rises, demand falls. If we plot this on the graph, we would indicate it by a movement from one point of the demand curve to another.

3.23 However, changes in other determinants of demand have the effect of shifting the entire demand curve to the left or right, as indicated by Figure 8.1(b). For example, suppose that the main curve in Figure 8.1(b) represents the demand for Product X. Now suppose that a new manufacturer enters the market with a rival product, Product Y, which is immediately perceived as very attractive. This has the effect of shifting the entire demand curve for Product X to the left, as indicated by the dotted line in Figure 8.1(b). What this means is that the level of demand for Product X is less than it used to be at all prices that the producer may charge.

3.24 There is a similar effect with supply curves. A change in price is plotted on the graph as a movement from one point of the supply curve to another: Figure 8.2(a). However, a change in any of the other determinants of supply is shown by a shift in the entire supply curve: Figure 8.2(b)

The interaction of supply and demand

3.25 Consumers want to pay as little as possible, but suppliers want to charge as much as possible. The two sides of the market have to compromise at some price between these two extremes. When the demand and supply curves are put together, **equilibrium price** is at the point of intersection and is the result of the interaction of demand and supply (refer back to Figure 8.3). It also ensures that demand and supply adjust until the quantities which consumers want to buy just equal the quantities which suppliers wish to sell, in a compromise which Adam Smith in his *Wealth of Nations* (1776) called 'the invisible hand'. In fact, there is a two-way relationship: price affects demand and supply; and demand and supply affect price.

Price elasticity of demand and supply

3.26 Price elasticity of demand is the degree of sensitivity of demand for a good to changes in the price of that good. Goods are described as 'inelastic' if the quantity of them demanded is relatively insensitive to the price charged. Typically such goods are basics, such as food, which people put at the top of their spending priorities. Conversely, demand is described as being 'elastic' where the quantity of a good demanded is relatively sensitive to a change in price. The phrase 'price elasticity of demand' is a bit long winded, so it is often shortened to 'elasticity of demand' or even PED.

3.27 Price elasticity is the proportionate change in demand divided by the proportionate change in the good's price. Although mathematically this can be defined in a number of ways, the most common formula is as follows.

$$PED = \frac{\text{Percentage change in quantity demanded}}{\text{Percentage change in price}}$$

Because an **increase** in price normally causes a **reduction** in the quantity demanded, the PED is normally negative. In fact this is so common that frequently the PED is stated without its minus sign, so beware!

3.28 As an example of this calculation, if PED for a certain good currently equals –2, how will sales be affected if price rises by 10 per cent? You should be able to see that there will be a fall of 20 per cent in the quantity demanded.

3.29 When PED > 1 (ie price elasticity of demand is greater than 1), demand is relatively elastic and the quantity demanded is very responsive to price changes; when PED < 1 (ie price elasticity of demand is less than 1), demand is relatively inelastic and the quantity demanded is not very responsive to price changes.

3.30 Note that if demand is said to be inelastic, this does not mean that there will be no change in quantity demanded when the price changes. It means that the consequent demand change will be **proportionately** smaller than the price change. If demand does not change at all after a price change, demand is said to be perfectly inelastic.

3.31 Price elasticity of demand will therefore be low for goods which are necessities or are habit forming because these have few substitutes in the perception of the consumer. Equally goods which have many substitutes and which represent a large proportion of consumer's expenditure have an elastic demand.

3.32 When demand is elastic, total revenue rises as price falls. This is because the quantity demanded is very responsive to price changes. A fall in the price gives rise to a **more** than proportionate rise in the quantity demanded. The net effect is that revenue (= price × quantity) rises.

3.33 Conversely, when demand is inelastic, total revenue falls as price falls. Here a fall in price causes a **less** than proportionate rise in quantity demanded, the result being a net fall in total revenue.

The relevance of elasticity to buyers

3.34 It is not an easy matter to estimate the elasticity of demand for a product. The judgment of expert analysts may be a helpful indicator. Customer surveys may also provide useful information. Some companies use field testing exercises to assess the effects of price changes on demand. In the last resort, though, it is not an exact science.

3.35 Despite this, buyers should not underestimate the usefulness of price elasticity. If a reasonable estimate can be formed of the elasticity of demand for a product, the information can be put to good use in a negotiation.

- If demand for a product is known to be inelastic, it may be unrealistic to hope for any price concessions from the supplier. The buyer should focus his negotiating effort on other areas.
- A buyer may be able to assess elasticity of demand for products of alternative suppliers. This can assist in making a choice between them.

3.36 Even if the supplier benefits from low price elasticity (enabling him to increase prices without losing business) it is not all bad news for the buyer. For one thing, the particular item may be only a small part of his total spend. For another, the buyer may be more interested in other factors, such as quality. Or the buying organisation may be so profitable that it can cope with price increases, and perhaps pass them on to its own customers.

4 Pricing and availability

4.1 Price is the amount of money that has to be paid to acquire a given product. Price is also a measure of the product's value.

4.2 Prices perform an economic function of major significance. So long as they are not artificially controlled, prices provide an economic mechanism by which goods and services are distributed among the large number of people desiring them. They also act as indicators of the strength of demand for different products and enable producers to respond accordingly.

4.3 This system is known as the price mechanism and is based on the principle that only by allowing prices to move freely will the supply of any given commodity match demand. If supply is excessive, prices will be low and production will be reduced; this will cause prices to rise until there is a balance of demand and supply. In the same way, if supply is inadequate, prices will be high, leading to an increase in production that in turn will lead to a reduction in prices until both supply and demand are in equilibrium.

The role of purchasing

4.4 Purchasing has a responsibility in ensuring the right quantity, of the right quality, at the right time, to the right place, for the right price. Pricing and availability are therefore fundamental to meeting the purchasing department's objectives.

4.5 We have seen earlier in this chapter that economic factors, often outside the purchaser's control, will influence both the price and availability of a product. The challenge facing the purchaser is how to ensure continuation of supply and stability of price in a volatile market.

4.6 Purchasers in a particular business discipline will, over time, understand the mechanics of their market in regard to pricing and availability. The main areas to consider are as follows.

- The main suppliers: does one supplier dominate the market? Are there alternative suppliers we can use? Are there alternative (substitute) products available?
- The factors influencing price: are prices controlled by suppliers? Are changes in global commodity prices causing prices to rise? Is the value of our currency falling, making imports more expensive?
- The factors influencing availability: is there a global or local shortage of supply? Is the shortage of goods due to disruptions (such as strikes) in our own country? Is the shortage caused by stockpiling of goods for speculative reasons?

4.7 To answer these and other questions satisfactorily the purchaser needs to develop a deep understanding of his particular market and the internal and external factors that influence it. For example, if we are aware that there are likely to be supply problems in the near future we can take action; if we are aware that prices will increase in the future and understand why, we can do something about it or at least budget for it.

4.8 There are a number of options open to the purchaser to ensure price stability. However, they are not always practical in all situations. For example, if we are buying commodities or semi-manufactured items we can consider buying in advance, fixing a price with the supplier now for delivery at a future date.

4.9 If we are concerned about movements in the exchange rate we can consider buying the overseas supplier's currency now (using the spot rate – the rate ruling at the time) for payment in the future. Banks will be able to offer advice as well as these services.

4.10 Of course there are risks with approaches such as these. Firstly, the price of the item might fall, rather than increasing as anticipated. Secondly, we may be tying up capital that could be used by the company for other purposes. Purchasers need to decide using their own acquired knowledge and the knowledge of those around them.

4.11 By forming a closer relationship with our suppliers we can expect preferential treatment in time of shortage of materials, particularly if we include that proviso in our contract with them.

4.12 By using these methods and other similar methods we can help ensure availability or help ensure price stability. Market knowledge, coupled with understanding of the laws of supply and demand, allows us to anticipate future problems and take advance precautions against them.

Chapter summary

- A market is a 'place' where buyers and sellers interact. A market economy is one in which economic choices (what to produce, how, for whom, and at what price) are made by the market via the market mechanism: supply and demand.
- Demand (the amount of goods consumers want to buy) usually falls as prices rise, in a downward demand curve. Supply (the amount of goods firms want to produce) usually rises as prices rise, in an upward supply curve. The market eventually stabilises at a price where supply equals demand (equilibrium price).
- The demand for a product is determined by such factors as its price and quality, income levels, availability and price of substitutes and complements, customer tastes and advertising.
- The supply of a product is determined by such factors as its price, cost levels, random uncontrollable factors, level of technology, new entrants to the market, and availability and price of complements.
- Prices have a key impact on availability of supplies. It is one of the tasks of purchasers to ensure that there is consistent availability of required supplies.

Self-test questions

Numbers in brackets refer to the paragraphs where you can check your answers.

1 Define micro economics. (1.1)

2 A typical demand curve slopes upwards from left to right. True or false? (Figure 8.1)

3 What is meant by the equilibrium price for a product? (2.7)

4 A rise in the price of a substitute causes a rise in the demand for the basic product. True or false? (3.7)

5 How can supply be affected by uncontrollable factors? (3.17)

6 Distinguish between a movement along a demand curve and a shift in the curve. (3.22, 3.23)

7 When demand is elastic, total revenue rises as price falls. True or false? (3.32)

8 What are the main market factors that purchasers must monitor in relation to pricing and availability? (4.6)

CHAPTER 9

The Impact of Market Factors

Assessment criteria and indicative content

3.3 Describe how market factors impact on the procurement and supply activities of an organisation

- The level of competition: perfect competition, imperfect competition, oligopoly, duopoly and monopolies
- The impact of demand on sales
- Market growth and decline
- Competitive forces on organisations

Section headings

1 The level of competition
2 Perfect competition
3 Monopoly
4 Monopolistic (imperfect) competition
5 Oligopoly
6 Demand, growth and decline
7 Competitive forces on organisations

1 The level of competition

Market structure

1.1 The term 'market structure' refers to different *levels of competition* that might be found in a market. Customer spending power (in product markets) and resources or factors of production (in factor markets) are inevitably limited. This means that if there is more than one player in a market, they will have to compete for a share of the market. The nature and intensity of that competition will influence the behaviour and performance of the players in the market – and their purchasing strategies.

1.2 There are four basic market structures.

- **Perfect competition** is a theoretical construct, which is never really achieved in practice – but is useful for analysing the effects of competition. It represents a set of conditions in which no supplier (among many) has the market power to influence the price of a good: there will be only one price for the good, determined by total market supply and demand.
- **Monopoly** is another theoretical construct at the opposite end of the scale: a situation in which no competition exists at all, because a single producer supplies the whole market. This producer has ultimate market power, and can (unless regulated) decide what it will charge for the good.
- **Monopolistic competition** is a form of 'imperfect' competition. It describes a situation where there is competition between a large number of suppliers producing goods which are

slightly different (or differentiated) in some way: in specification, or packaging, or consumer perception, say. These differences may allow suppliers to set slightly varying prices for a good.

- **Oligopoly** is another form of 'imperfect' competition. It describes a situation where there is competition between a small number of large suppliers of differentiated goods. Such suppliers have considerable market power to set prices, but will be reluctant to engage in unilateral price rises (risk of losing market share) or cuts (risk of creating a price war). Instead, they will usually work together to keep prices stable.

1.3 These structures can be seen as a continuum from very competitive markets to markets in which there is no competition at all: Figure 9.1.

Figure 9.1 *The competitive spectrum*

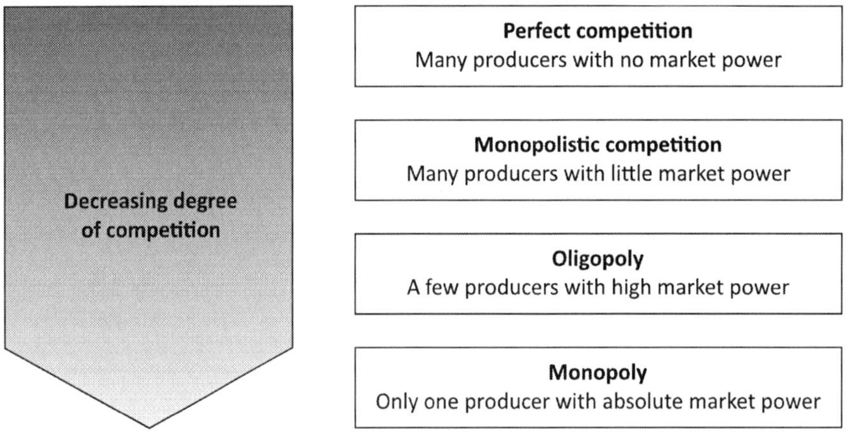

2 Perfect competition

Market conditions creating a perfectly competitive market

2.1 Perfect competition is an 'ideal' situation in which no player in the market has market power to influence the price of a good. The market conditions which need to be fulfilled to bring this situation about are as follows.

- There are many buyers and sellers: each is so small relative to the total market that its actions cannot affect the market. For example, there is no buyer able to buy such large quantities that it could influence the market price.
- The goods being marketed are 'homogeneous': in other words, identical.
- 'Perfect information' about the market is available to all parties.
- There is no 'economic friction': the same market factors (eg risk, storage and transport costs) affect all parties equally.
- There are no 'barriers to entry or exit': firms can choose to enter or leave the market without cost. (We will discuss this further below.)
- There is 'perfect mobility': producers can use resources for any purpose, and consumers can purchase from any supplier, without incurring switching costs.

2.2 What this essentially means is that no supplier or buyer will have power to influence the price of the good in the market. If one supplier tries to charge a higher price than the others, everyone will know (because of perfect information) – and there will be no barrier to consumers simply switching to another supplier (because the goods are identical and all other factors are equal). All firms will have to toe the line of market price, which will be determined by supply and demand in the total market: they are said to be *price takers* – accepting the 'going rate' for the good.

2.3 Market price will generally settle at a level which allows suppliers to make 'normal profits': that is, sufficient revenue to cover their costs, plus a margin of profit sufficient for them to stay in business. If a firm earns less than this, in the absence of barriers to exit, it will simply leave the market. If a firm earns more than this ('abnormal profits'), everyone will know: in the absence of barriers to entry, other firms will enter the market seeking to share in the supra-normal profits that are available – and with more competition and higher supply, prices will fall, returning profits to the normal level.

Barriers to entry and exit

2.4 *Barriers to entry* are factors which reduce the attractiveness or profitability of a market to potential new competitors from outside, and therefore reduce the likelihood that they will enter the market. In perfect competition, no such barriers exist – but in oligopoly and monopoly markets, firms will have an interest in *erecting* such barriers (if they do not already exist) in order to protect their power and profits.

2.5 The main barriers to entry include the following.

- Economies of scale and other cost advantages for established competitors (eg bulk purchasing and production economies, lower marketing costs, no learning curve, preferential access to necessary inputs), allowing them to squeeze out new entrants with a price war if necessary
- High capital investment requirements in order to enter the market
- Product differentiation and brand identity: hard-to-imitate offerings with costly-to-counter market profile and customer loyalty. Established competitors can afford to spend heavily on advertising, the cost of which will be spread over a large number of units sold: newer, smaller entrants may struggle to advertise at levels required to create awareness and woo customers from existing players.
- Switching costs (eg time, inconvenience, unfamiliarity with the new product, perhaps cost of getting out of existing contracts) and customer loyalty to existing brands, hindering new product trial and adoption by the market
- Existing players' control over supply and distribution channels (perhaps on a selective or exclusive basis which would hinder competitors)
- Existing players' control over a natural resource for which no close substitutes exist (eg ownership of or access to minerals or forests)
- Restricted labour or skill supply (eg the provision of accountancy and legal services being restricted to members of appropriate professional bodies)
- Government policy and legislative barriers: for example, laws protecting established players' intellectual property (eg design patents and copyrights) or physical property (such as mineral or fishing rights).

2.6 *Barriers to exit* are factors which make it difficult for an existing supplier to *leave* an industry, if it proves unattractive or unprofitable. Here are some barriers to exit.

- A lack of assets with significant break-up, re-sale or re-use value, so that the firm will not be able to realise any value from them (other than by continuing to use them)
- The cost of redundancy payments, if workers have to be laid off as a result of the closure or change of activity
- Effects on other divisions or activities maintained by the firm: loss of morale and/or strategic

direction due to the divestment, loss of complementary products (which may have an impact on the sale of other items in the product range), loss of managerial talent (if not transferred to other divisions)
- Reputational damage, as a result of factory closures, product withdrawals and so on – which may impact on the firm's other product lines
- Corporate social responsibility and/or government pressure to maintain employment and the production of essential goods and services (even if they are unprofitable).

Are there any perfectly competitive markets?

2.7 There are some markets which arguably come close to being perfectly competitive. The stock markets and foreign exchange markets are examples. There are many operators in the market; each company's shares and each country's currency are identical; there is an emphasis on transparency and information is transmitted very quickly to all market participants; and transaction costs are similar for all operators. However, some operators (eg large pension funds or insurance companies) do have market power; and there are barriers to entry (eg in the form of minimum authorised share capital).

The implications of perfect competition for procurement

2.8 Perfect competition means that there will be literally nothing to choose between one supplier and another. Buyers have perfect information about all suppliers' prices, and since all offerings are identical, they are perfectly free to switch suppliers to secure the market rate. Any supplier who charges above the market price, or seeks abnormal profit margins, will quickly have to come into line in order to stay competitive. Buyers may also seek to play suppliers against each other to secure prices below market rate: it doesn't matter if a supplier is driven out of business, because there are plenty of others – and no costs of exit for the supplier.

2.9 Even where a market is slightly less than perfect, there will be the same incentive for suppliers to compete on price, and this will be to buyers' advantage. Given identical offerings, and low switching costs, buyers have the market power to 'shop around'.

2.10 From the buyer's viewpoint, the *downside* of perfect competition is that there may be many buyers as well as many sellers. Small buyers will lack market power to influence suppliers on price. If they don't like the terms of business, suppliers will know they can sell their goods to plenty of other buyers instead.

3 Monopoly

Features of a monopoly

3.1 In its 'ideal' form, a monopoly exists when one producer supplies the whole market. The conditions for a monopoly are as follows.

- Only one supplier of the good exists. It may be a single organisation, or a group of producers acting together to control supply (eg a cartel such as the Organisation of Petroleum Exporting Countries, or OPEC).
- There are barriers to entry, preventing other firms from entering the market (eg high set-up costs, high customer loyalty to the existing producer, or the existing producer monopolising sources of supply and distribution channels).
- There are no close substitutes for the good being produced (which would enable buyers to switch).

3.2 If these conditions are met, the monopolist essentially controls supply, and has absolute power to determine the price of the good in its market: it is said to be a *price maker.* It is this feature which can lead to consumers being over-charged, which is why monopoly markets are usually regulated, as we will see.

3.3 Control over supply and price enables monopolists to achieve and sustain abnormal profits, because there are no competitors to increase supply (lowering prices and therefore eroding profits).

Price discrimination

3.4 A monopolist may be able to operate *price discrimination:* charging different prices for the same good in different markets or market segments. So, for example, the same train ticket may be more expensive in peak commuter hours than in off-peak hours – or if booked in person rather than online. Consumers with higher disposable income will be willing to pay more for the same good or service than less affluent consumers (perhaps even perceiving that the higher price tag means better quality).

3.5 In order for price discrimination to be possible, the firm must be able to identify different market segments with different demand conditions, so that different prices are tolerated by each. The higher price will be charged to the market where the demand is relatively 'inelastic' (that is, where demand is not sensitive to price changes) and the lower price where it is relatively 'elastic' (where demand is sensitive to price). There must also be no possibility of resale by one consumer to another, so people charged the lower price can't go out and resell the good to those being charged the higher price, possibly undercutting the original provider.

3.6 You might think of price discrimination as 'discriminatory' in a bad sense, exploiting some consumers by charging them more for the same good. However, it has some benefits for both the supplier and the consumer.

- It allows efficient resource usage: lower prices can be used to stimulate sales in 'off-peak' periods, to shift unused stock (or fill last-minute vacancies) – and hence to smooth out fluctuations in demand.
- It takes into account affordability for different groups of consumers, allowing less affluent groups equal access to goods and services, and charging more to groups who are able and willing to pay more.

Regulation of monopoly

3.7 The power exercised by a monopoly supplier is clearly very great, and there is a danger that the monopolist will abuse that power by charging excessive prices, or reducing the quality of service, or both. To protect consumers, most governments put legislation in place to regulate monopolies, and also potential mergers which might result in monopolies (eg if there are currently only a small number of suppliers and they are proposing to merge their operations into a single company).

3.8 A monopoly may be considered to endanger the public interest if its effect is: to hinder effective competition; to damage consumer interests (eg by unfairly raising prices or reducing quality); to limit development; or to distort the distribution of industry and employment. It is these possibilities that governments are concerned to monitor and regulate.

The implications of monopoly for procurement

3.9 The main concern for buyers will be a *monopoly supplier*'s absolute power in the market: there will be no opportunity for the buyer to take its business elsewhere, so the monopolist will be able to dictate terms and conditions of trade. The only alternatives will be to seek substitute goods or services which would serve the same purpose, *or* to seek new supply markets, perhaps internationally. This may even be a helpful spur to strategic thinking and innovation.

3.10 Prices will generally be higher in the absence of competition, and the buyer will not be able to exert pressure to reduce prices – nor to improve quality or service levels. Its business is likely to represent only a small part of the supplier's revenue. However, monopolists enjoy *economies of scale:* that is, cost savings arising from their large size. Large-scale operations make greater use of advanced machinery and efficient mass production techniques; are able to access finance more cheaply; are able to benefit from bulk discounts on purchases; and so on. Some of these cost savings *may* be passed on to buyers in the form of reasonable prices – although this may have to be achieved by regulation. Regulation may limit the prices that monopolists are allowed to charge, for example.

3.11 Another issue of concern is that buyers may be unable to specify their exact supply requirements, since the monopoly supplier has little incentive to tailor its product range to the needs of a large number of potential buyers. There may be little or no choice, customisation or innovation – and this might be a serious problem for buyers whose own competitive market is highly specialised or fast-changing. Again, however, this is not *necessarily* the case: monopolists may have more resources to invest in customisation, flexibility and innovation, with the incentive of even higher profits.

3.12 You should also be able to think of the issues raised by the reverse set of circumstances: the position of suppliers faced with a *monopoly buyer,* with absolute bargaining power. There will be considerable risk for suppliers forced to adapt their technology, processes and offerings to the needs of a single customer. If they lose the monopoly's custom, there may be few immediate alternative markets. Suppliers may be driven out of business when large customers, on whom they are highly dependent, squeeze their prices beyond the point of sustainability, or terminate the supply relationship.

4 Monopolistic (imperfect) competition

Features of monopolistic competition

4.1 'Monopolistic competition' is not to be confused with 'monopoly'. It is a form of imperfect competition, arising where the following market conditions apply.

- There are many suppliers (though not as many as in perfect competition)
- Goods are *not* homogeneous: each supplier produces a good which is slightly differentiated from its competitors. (This means that each supplier is a monopoly for its own 'version' of a good – hence 'monopolistic' – but faces competition in the market for the good in general. Apple is a monopoly producer of iPods, but there are many types of MP3 players on the market.)
- There are barriers to entry (such as customer loyalty and brand strength), but not sufficient to prevent other firms from entering the market in the long term.

4.2 Products may be different in their technical specifications or performance, or differentiation may be added to the total offering: better after-sales service, say, or longer warranty periods. The difference may also lie in the perception of consumers, rather than in the product itself: product 'positioning' is the name given in marketing to consumers' perception of a product's values and attributes in comparison to competitors. Consumers can be encouraged to develop a preference for, and ultimately a loyalty to, a product through distinctive branding, packaging and promotion – even if the product itself is identical to its competitors. (Why is an iPod different from another functionally similar MP3 player, for example?)

4.3 Differentiation gives firms a degree of market power, as (unlike in a perfectly competitive market, where goods are identical) consumers may develop a preference for certain features and products, allowing suppliers to charge a little above market price without losing all their customers. In fact, it may be possible to *increase* demand for a product by raising prices slightly, where consumers perceive this to be a sign of high-quality or high-status goods. Similarly, a firm which lowers its prices slightly will not necessarily benefit from increased demand, because many consumers will remain loyal to their preferred brand.

4.4 With the ability to sustain slightly above-market prices, firms may be able to make modest super-normal profits in the short term – although in the long run, super-normal profits will still attract new competitors, which will bring profits back into line.

4.5 It could be argued that imperfect competition is wasteful of resources, compared to perfect competition, because of the investment in promotion and other forms of differentiation. However, this can be seen as the price society has to pay for choice.

4.6 Monopolistic competition is very common: you should be able to think of many examples, from clothes to cereals to cars.

Implications of monopolistic competition for procurement

4.7 These are probably the market conditions you will face most commonly in your professional work as a purchaser. They create a more complicated market than either of the theoretical extremes, in that suppliers will compete along a range of different dimensions: not just price, but non-price criteria such as quality, variety, flexibility, speed of delivery, service and so on. Buyers will need to have a clear idea of what price and non-price criteria are most important for a given purchase category in a given set of circumstances, in order to select the right suppliers for their needs.

4.8 The balance of power between buyers and sellers will also be more complex: buyers will have the power to switch brands, but not without cost (researching other suitable suppliers, losing their 'preferred' brand and so on). There may be room for negotiation of mutually satisfying purchase contracts and relationships, achieving a balance between the needs of both sides.

5 Oligopoly

Features of oligopoly

5.1 An oligopoly is a situation in which a small number of large producers dominate a market in which products are differentiated. This may sound like monopolistic competition, only with fewer players – but the number of players makes a significant difference. With so few firms in the market, each having a significant share of the total market, actions by any one will have direct consequences for all the others. No firm in the market can take decisions independently of the others, because of the likelihood that competitors will respond. (You may sometimes meet references to an oligopoly where the suppliers are just two in number: a **duopoly**.)

5.2 This creates a distinctive tactical climate.

- There is little *price competition* in the market. Firms have similar market knowledge, so their cost structures and prices will be broadly similar. Moreover, a firm will be reluctant to lower prices unilaterally, because competitors will simply do the same to protect their market share – creating price wars in which the whole industry will lose out. And it will be reluctant to *raise* prices unilaterally, because if competitors *don't* do the same, it may lose market share.
- Competition usually takes *non-price forms*: product differentiation supported by branding, advertising, promotions (special offers) and added-value benefits (eg after-sales service, loyalty reward programmes and so on). Think about how the major supermarket or petrol station chains try to stimulate sales and customer loyalty, for example.
- Market prices tend to be set by non-competitive means, in order to maintain price stability and avoid damaging price wars. One approach is that a dominant firm takes the lead in setting the market price, and smaller firms follow suit: this is called *price leadership.* Another approach is for firms in the market to agree between them what prices will be: this is called 'collusion'. (We will discuss it further below.)
- Firms often maintain high barriers to new competitors entering the market, in order to preserve the *status quo* and their market share: for example, by strong branding, controlling channels of supply and distribution, and preventing newcomers from joining cartels.

5.3 Oligopolists have a great deal of market power, by virtue of their size. Super-normal profits are therefore achievable, depending on the strength of competitors and the level of prices that are sustainable in the market.

5.4 There are many examples of oligopoly markets, including the tobacco, brewing, confectionery and toy industries – in all of which, the top few firms in the industry have a market share over 85%.

Collusion in oligopoly markets

5.5 There is a temptation for the few firms in an oligopolistic market to join forces to keep out new competitors and fix prices. This can be done by various forms of collusion.

5.6 A **price cartel** or **price ring** is formed when a group of oligopoly firms join forces to agree – and therefore control – output quotas (the amount that will be produced) and market prices. Each participant can increase its profits, if all major competitors charge the same price: potentially, the same high price as a monopoly might be able to charge.

5.7 In order for a cartel to be successful, it must include most or all of the major producers and distributors (in order to avoid price competition). There must not be close substitutes for the product (in order to avoid customers' switching in response to high prices), and demand cannot be too price sensitive (so that demand will not fall so much, in response to high prices, that the producers' income will be reduced rather than raised). In addition, the participants must be able to agree on their share of the total supply to the market (which dictates their proportion of the revenue and profits available): this is sometimes the hardest hurdle of all.

5.8 The best known cartel is OPEC, which controls most of the oil production in the world. However, EU treaty provisions, the UK Competition Act and the Enterprise Act 2002, and other legislation in countries throughout the world, now outlaw cartels. In a well-known 2003 case, for example, a group of ten businesses was found to have illegally entered price-fixing agreements in relation to the sale of replica football kit, around the time of the Euro 2000 Championship (the 'duplicate kit cartel').

5.9 There are also various forms of *informal price collusion*, including the following.

- Systems of 'recommended retail prices', with sellers discouraged from selling at lower or differentiated prices.
- Price leadership by one firm, which is then followed by others in the market.

5.10 Informal collusion is also outlawed in most countries, because its effect is to reduce or distort competition between firms, to the detriment of consumers. Even so, it goes on: collusion includes not just explicit agreements but implicit 'understandings' and even competitors watching each others' pricing decisions and following suit. These kinds of behaviour can be difficult to control.

5.11 Apart from collusive agreements being against the best interests of the consumer, and subject to law and public scrutiny (with the risk of financial penalties and reputational damage), they are also tricky for the participants. This is because of the temptation for cartel members to break ranks for short-term profit-taking. Nevertheless, the market is best served in the long run by price stability, so competition is usually focused on non-price differentiation and promotion.

Implications of oligopoly for procurement

5.12 Because of the non-homogeneity of goods in the market, buyers will (as with monopolistic competition) have a degree of product choice. Because of the oligopoly's avoidance of price competition, particular emphasis will have to be placed on getting the best possible value for money through a combination of non-price factors. If buyers cannot negotiate on price, they will need to use whatever buyer power they have to secure the best possible service, support and other added value benefits.

5.13 In an oligopoly supply market, suppliers have strong market power by virtue of their size and small number – and any type of formal or informal collusion will add to their bargaining strength and reduce that of buyers. As with a monopoly, oligopoly suppliers can therefore charge high prices – but will benefit from economies of scale which they *may* choose to pass on to buyers. Buyers may seek to enhance their bargaining power in various ways: by developing their negotiating skills; perhaps by consolidating their purchases; or by banding together in a buying consortium with other purchasing organisations, so that they can offer a larger volume of business to a given supplier.

5.14 For a supplier dealing with an oligopoly *buyer*, the position will be reversed. The buyer will represent a potentially large volume of business (although it may divide its demand among a large number of suppliers), allowing the supplier economies of scale and standardisation. On the other hand, bargaining power will lie with the buyer, enabling it to force prices down and raise quality and service (in the interests of its own competitive advantage).

Round-up of market structures

5.15 Here is a summary and comparison of the key features of the four market structures: Table 9.1.

Table 9.1 *Comparison of market structures*

PERFECT COMPETITION	MONOPOLISTIC COMPETITION	OLIGOPOLY	MONOPOLY
Very many small suppliers	Many slightly larger suppliers	Few large suppliers	One supplier
No market power	Little market power	High market power	Absolute market power
Homogeneous goods: suppliers' products are interchangeable	Differentiated goods: suppliers' products are close substitutes	Differentiated goods: degree of substitution variable	No substitutes
One market price: suppliers are 'price takers'	Price competition	Seeking of price stability by price leadership or collusion	Price set by one 'price maker': potential for price discrimination
Normal profits	Small abnormal profits, short term	Abnormal profits, depending on competition	Abnormal profits
No advertising or branding (everyone knows all goods identical)	Heavy advertising and branding > differentiation	Much advertising and branding, ie competition not based on price	Not much advertising or branding required (no competition)
No barriers to entry	No barriers to entry in the long run	Barriers to entry	Barriers to entry

6 Demand, growth and decline

The impact of demand on sales

6.1 Demand is the economic principle that describes a consumer's desire and willingness to pay a price for a specific good or service.

6.2 If a new mobile phone came on to the market, from a leading company and packed with new features, demand might well be very high. For marketing reasons over the long term the manufacturer would ensure that the price was reasonable. However, they are also aware that they could charge more, particularly when demand is strong. Think of tickets for concerts, shows and sporting events. Here demand can be so strong that a second market often opens up ('touts') selling at seemingly excessive prices to meet demand. The question is: are they selling at excessive prices or are they selling at a price that the market will bear (ie that customers are willing to pay)?

6.3 Businesses will often spend a great deal of money in order to determine the amount of demand the public has for its products and services. Incorrect estimations will either result in product left on the shelf or a shortage of product (unfulfilled demand).

6.4 The law of demand is simply that when the price of a good rises, the amount demanded falls, and when the price falls, the amount demanded rises. All other things being equal, when the price of a good rises, the amount of it demanded decreases. We saw this illustrated in the form of a demand curve in the previous chapter.

6.5 The law of demand is ingrained in our way of thinking about everyday things. Shoppers buy more strawberries when they are in season and the price is low. No one thinks, for example, that the way to sell a house that has been languishing on the market is to raise the asking price. Again, this shows an implicit awareness of the law of demand: the number of potential buyers for any given house varies inversely with the asking price.

6.6 When there is a close substitute for one firm's brand, a small percentage increase in that firm's price may lead to a large percentage cut in the amount of the firm's good demanded. In such a case, economists say that the demand for the good is highly elastic. On the other hand, when there are few good substitutes for a firm's product, the firm might be able to raise its price substantially with only a small decrease in the quantity demanded resulting. In such a case, demand is said to be highly inelastic.

6.7 It is not just price that affects the quantity demanded. Income affects it too. As real income rises, people buy more of some goods (which economists call 'normal goods') and less of others (called 'inferior goods'). Buses and trains are classic examples of inferior goods. That is why, in highly developed economies, the usage of both of these modes of travel declined so dramatically as post-war incomes rose and more people could afford motorcycles and cars.

6.8 Another influence on demand is the price of substitutes. When the price of BMW M5 rises, all else being equal, the quantity demanded falls and the demand for Nissan GT-R, a substitute, rises. The price of complements, or goods that are used together, will impact demand. When the price of fuel rises, the demand for cars falls.

Market growth and decline

6.9 Economic growth is the increase in the amount of goods and services produced by an economy over a period of time. It is conventionally measured as a percentage increase or decrease in the gross domestic product (GDP). Growth will usually be calculated in 'real' terms (ie after adjusting for the effects of price inflation).

6.10 GDP has become a focus in recent years as many world economies struggle to stay out of recession. Economies that show negative growth for three consecutive quarters are said to be in recession. Growth figures as applied to european economies in recent years indicate no growth or limited growth as indicated by the GDP figures. In other areas of the world, such as China, growth has been substantial over the same period.

6.11 Economists distinguish between short-term economic changes in production and long-term economic growth. Short-term variation in economic growth is termed the business cycle. The business cycle consists of good periods and bad periods that occur over a period of time. The most recent example was the global boom of 2002 onwards that ended with the bust of 2008.

6.12 Economists attribute the ups and downs of the business cycle to a number of causes that include the overproduction of goods with resultant large inventories that are difficult to sell, increased access to credit resulting in high levels of debt, and shocks such as wars and political upheavals.

6.13 Market growth is heavily influenced by both economic growth and the business cycle. In the boom years consumers have ready money to spend and in the lean years they refrain from buying. No market is exempt from this.

6.14 Innovation, changes in market structure and changes in income distribution are all factors in economic and market growth and decline. If a company innovates successfully and brings a new product to market it may succeed when others are failing. If one or a number of companies fall out of the market it leaves a gap for others to fill and increased wealth for a small number of people again provides opportunities.

7 Competitive forces on organisations

7.1 Some of the key texts on competition and competitive advantage were written in the 1980s by Professor Michael Porter. He suggested that 'competition in an industry is rooted in its underlying economics' (as we have already seen) and that 'competitive forces exist that go well beyond the established combatants in a particular industry'. Porter developed a framework which argues that the extent of competition in an industry – and therefore its attractiveness or potential profitability to any given player within it – depends on the interaction of five forces in the organisation's industry environment.

Porter's five forces model

7.2 Although the *five forces model,* as it is called, is not mentioned explicitly in your syllabus, it is an important tool for understanding markets. We will therefore summarise its main features here.

7.3 Five forces determine the extent of competition in an industry: Figure 9.2.

Figure 9.2 *Porter's five forces model*

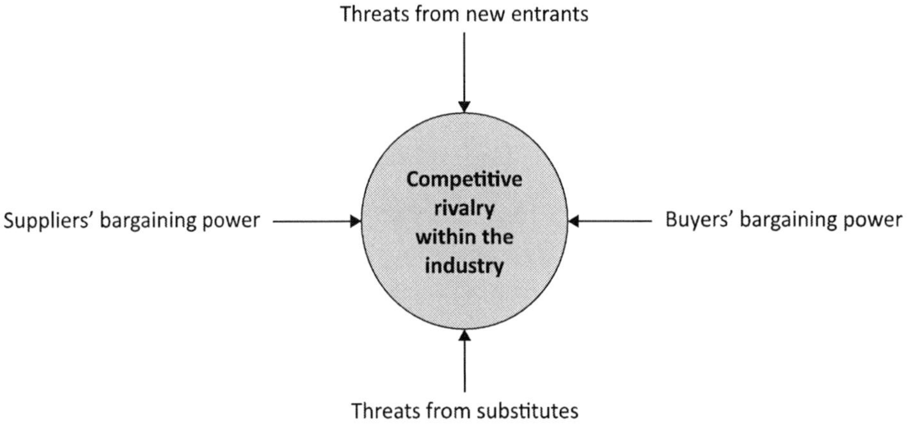

7.4 **Potential new entrants** to an industry may make it more competitive by: expanding supply (without necessarily increasing market demand); striving to penetrate the market and build market share, perhaps by innovating or competing aggressively; and increasing costs, as they bid for factors of production. It is therefore in the interests of existing competitors to deter new entrants. The strength of the threat from new entrants will vary from industry to industry, according to the strength of barriers to entry (discussed earlier) – and the response of existing competitors to any new entrant. (If existing players typically respond to new competitors by competing aggressively on price, a prospective entrant might think twice about whether entry will be profitable...)

7.5 **Substitute products** are alternative products that serve the same purpose (eg postal services, courier services, fax machines, email), making it easy for buyers to switch, and therefore limiting the price that a company can charge for its products. There is a particular risk in that a company may not see a substitute coming, if it results from innovation. Where there are plenty of substitutes available, demand for a product is likely to be relatively price sensitive: buyers are more likely to switch in response to price rises (or price cuts by competitors). Improved price or value positioning in substitute products is therefore a significant threat.

7.6 **Buyer power** may make an industry more competitive by enabling buyers (customers) to: force down prices; bargain for higher quality or improved services; or play competing providers against each other. Porter suggested that buyers are particularly powerful in the following situations.

- They are limited in number and/or large in size, relative to supplying firms.
- Their spend is a high proportion of suppliers' revenue (but not a high proportion of their own spend, since this will make them dependent on the supplier).
- Products and services are undifferentiated, or there are substitute products, making it easy to switch suppliers.
- There is potential for 'backward integration' (ie buyers can own or control their suppliers: a book publisher taking over a printing company, say).

7.7 **Supplier power** (as we saw in the case of oligopolists and monopolists) is generally exercised to raise prices, squeezing buyers' profits (especially if they are unable to recover their cost increases by raising their own prices). Suppliers are particularly powerful in the following situations.

- They are limited in number and/or large in size, relative to buying firms.
- There are few substitute products and/or the supplier's product (and/or service) is highly differentiated.
- The volume purchased by the buyer or industry is not important to the supplier.
- The supplier's product is an important component in the buyer's business.
- The switching cost for buyers is high (eg because of investment in the relationship with a particular supplier, or contract penalties for switching).
- There is potential for 'forward integration' (ie suppliers can own or control their buyers: a clothing manufacturer opening retail stores, say).

7.8 The **intensity of rivalry** among current competitors may range, as we have seen, from collusion between competitors (in order to maintain and share the profits available in the industry) to the other extreme of aggressive competitive strategies such as innovation, price wars and promotional battles, where one firm's gain is another firm's loss. Rivalry is likely to be more intense in the following situations.

- There are many equally-balanced competitors.
- There is a slow rate of industry growth. (If the 'pie' isn't getting larger, the only way firms can grow will be to compete for a bigger 'slice'.)
- There is a lack of product and service differentiation.
- There are high fixed costs of production, since firms need higher revenue to cover them and make a profit.
- There are high barriers to exit, so it is less costly to compete harder than to withdraw from the industry.

7.9 You might like to think about the mobile phone industry, for example, or the soft drinks industry (the famous 'Cola wars' between Pepsi and Coke). What makes competition in these industries so intense – and on what basis do the major players seek to compete (a) with potential new entrants and (b) with each other?

Industry structure

7.10 Porter also classified industry structures according to the amount and type of competition within them.

- **Fragmented industries** are 'populated by a large number of small and medium-sized companies' and characterised by 'the absence of market leaders with the power to shape industry events'. You should be able to see how this corresponds to the market structure of perfect or monopolistic competition. An example of a fragmented industry might be hairdressing (since there are few large chains of salons).
- **Concentrated industries** are dominated by a small number of large competitors, which are able to exercise a significant influence over the market. You should be able to see how this corresponds to the market structure of oligopoly.

7.11 Industries may become fragmented over time, if their markets are attractive to smaller firms. This may be the case if barriers to entry are low, or there are few economies of scale to be exploited by larger firms; if innovation and flexibility are required in response to changing or fluctuating demand; if 'local' contacts, differentiation and reputation are important; or if the market itself is fragmented into small segments of customers with distinct tastes or needs (separate niche markets not worth the while of a large organisation to pursue). You might like to think about which of these conditions apply to the increasing fragmentation of the media and publishing industry, for example, with the availability of satellite and digital TV, web-based publishing and so on.

7.12 On the other hand, industries may become (or remain) concentrated, if conditions favour fewer, larger players: there are high barriers to entry, high costs of staying in business and competing, and/or good economies of scale available (where it is cheaper to purchase, produce, distribute and market goods in bulk). There may be consolidation of smaller competitors into fewer, larger ones, through mergers and acquisitions (although the larger resulting groups or chains may retain the distinctive features and markets of their component parts, eg by retaining different brands). A standardised product or service offering may become preferred to smaller, more customised competitors, enabling customers' needs to be fulfilled by fewer firms: think about large fast food chains and supermarkets, for example.

7.13 Porter also noted the existence of **emerging industries**: new or re-formed industries which have not yet settled into established patterns of competition. These may be created by technological innovation (eg creating electronic publishing and music industries) or social change (eg creating eco-friendly industries such as reverse logistics, and waste storage and recycling).

7.14 Emerging industries pose distinctive problems for organisations active within them, because of early barriers to entry (technology development, access to materials, problems obtaining funding, problems establishing a market) and uncertainty about the market and competition. Internal capabilities may have to be developed (including purchasing, in contexts where supply markets may not yet be established) and external environmental factors may be unfamiliar.

7.15 Emerging markets may also require a different approach to competition. If a company is first into an emerging market (eg discovering and patenting a new technology), it may choose *not* to maintain barriers to entry, in order to establish a monopoly, but to *encourage* competition (eg by licensing the technology to competitors), in order to co-opt other firms in building the profile and size of the market.

Monitoring competitors

7.16 Competitors are an important part of the external micro (market and industry) environment of purchasing.

- An organisation's strategies and products will, to an extent, be influenced by the need to gain or maintain an advantage over competitors in the market. Managers will attempt to predict what competitors will do, in order proactively to counter threats (or exploit opportunities) arising from their plans. So, for example, purchasers may need to monitor competitors' materials costs and quality, in order for their own purchasing and products to stay competitive.
- Competitors may be used as benchmarks for key competencies that are valued by the market. The organisation may measure its customer service, quality management or procurement efficiency, say, against the standards set by key competitors or market leaders.
- Competitors may seek advantage by controlling supply and distribution channels, eg by forming preferential relationships with suppliers or distributors, or negotiating exclusive supply and distribution contracts. An organisation's purchasers are therefore in direct competition with competitors' purchasers, especially where supplies are limited or scarce.

7.17 **Competitor analysis** is therefore a key component of environmental analysis. It involves analysing competitors' goals, capabilities (strengths and weaknesses), strategies (on what basis is it aiming to compete: price, product differentiation, niche markets?) and likely response to environmental threats and opportunities. Purchasers may, for example, need to look at competitors' relationships with key suppliers; whether they have (or may be able to obtain) control over sources of key or scarce supplies; how well they are able to control or reduce purchasing costs (enabling greater profitability and/or price competition); and so on.

Chapter summary

- Market structure refers to different forms and amounts of competition in a market.
- There are four basic market structures: perfect competition (many producers with no market power); monopolistic competition (many producers with some market power due to differentiation); oligopoly (a few large producers with high market power); and monopoly (only one producer with absolute market power).
- Each market structure depends on particular market conditions (number of suppliers and buyers, homogeneity or differentiation of goods, barriers to entry and so on).
- Each has particular characteristics: one market price in perfect competition; differentiation in monopolistic competition; competitive tactics and collusion in oligopoly; and absolute market power in monopoly.
- Each has advantages and/or disadvantages for a purchaser. You should revise these areas in detail.
- Porter's five forces model suggests that the extent of competition in a given industry environment is determined by: potential market entrants (and barriers to entry); substitute products; buyer power; supplier power; and the intensity of rivalry between competing firms.

Self-test questions

Numbers in brackets refer to paragraphs where you can check your answers

1 List the four market structures in order of *increasing* competition. (1.2, Figure 9.1)

2 List the conditions for perfect competition. (2.1)

3 What is price discrimination? (3.4)

4 How might products in imperfectly competitive markets be differentiated? (4.2)

5 What tactics are typically used by oligopoly suppliers? (5.2)

6 What are the advantages and disadvantages of dealing with (a) an oligopoly supplier and (b) an oligopoly customer? (5.12–5.14)

7 When do (a) buyers and (b) suppliers have more power in an industry? (7.6, 7.7)

Subject Index